DRIVING ACROSS
AMERICA

Tales from my life on the open road

Inspiring stories, unique experiences, and a country full of amusing people

DRIVING ACROSS AMERICA

Tales from my life on the open road

Inspiring stories, unique experiences, and a country full of amusing people

BILL CLEVLEN

PUBLISHING CONCEPTS LLC

Copyright @ 2019 by Bill Clevlen
First Edition

All rights reserved. No part of this publication may
be reproduced, stored in any retrieval system,
or transmitted in any form or by any means,
mechanical, photocopying, recording, or otherwise,
without permission in writing from the publisher.

Book design by Cerutti Graphic Design

Manufactured in the United States of America

For more information, please contact:
Publishing Concepts LLC
6590 Scanlan Avenue
St. Louis MO 63139
www.PublishingConceptsLLC.com

ISBN 13: 978-1-933635-33-0

TRAVEL & TOURISM
1 2 3 4 5 6 7 8 9 10

DEDICATION

This book is dedicated to my Uncle Bill, a U.S. Marine
and WWII veteran, that I'm honored to be named after.
He absolutely loved America and I'd like to think
he'd be proud that my job is to remind people
how great of a place it is to call home.

ACKNOWLEDGMENTS

Big thanks to the loyal supporters of *Bill on the Road* who read my travel stories, watch my videos, or listen to me on radio stations around the U.S. This job is much more fun knowing you're out there.

Joe Clote, thanks for being a big fan and always offering encouragement.

To my assistant Pamela, for all of your hard work. You deserve a raise. (You're not getting one, but you definitely deserve one.)

Thank you, Dad, for being a good sport and letting me share some of our travel adventures. Even when they're embarrassing.

To my brother, Brian. Thank you for stealing enough license plates to make a beautiful cover for the book.

MORE TO EXPLORE...
Maxie is located near the American Genius Highway in Missouri!

MAXIE
WORLD'S LARGEST GOOSE
SUMNER, MO.

CONTENTS

Preface 1
It's A Small Country, After All 7
The Thrifty Barber 9
A Museum For Everything 11
Fire In The Hole 18
A Million-Dollar Roof 23
Cooperstown 25
Trick Or Treat 29
Dude...Slow Down 31
Come On Down 33
International Hero 35
The Candy Machine 39
Goats On The Roof 41
Tragedy And Humanity 43
Dad's Computer 50
Won't You Be My Neighbor? 55
Detour: Bill's Ultimate Road Trip Playlist 58
Detour: Top 10 Favorite Museums 61
Detour: Road Trip Q&A 65
Detour: Road Trip Fun Facts 68
South Dakota 72

CONTENTS

The Cracker Barrel Gold Card 77
Home Sweet Home 79
The Day I Spent In Prison 85
Expensive Junk 89
Road Quirk 92
Popeye's Hometown 95
She Doesn't Work Here Anymore 97
Old, Dirty, Bumpy Roads 101
Clydesdales For Christmas 105
100 Men Hall 107
Meeting The Muppets 111
It's Never As Bad As They Say It Is 115
Road Trip Trivia Answers 121
My Favorite Travel Apps 123
Index 126

Kansas City, I'm so in Love

MORE TO EXPLORE...

Many cities now have cool murals that make for great Instagram photos!

MORE TO EXPLORE...
Bond Falls is just one of nearly 300 waterfalls in Michigan's Upper Peninsula.

PREFACE

The most frequent line I hear from people who follow *Bill on the Road* is, "You have such a dream job." In fact, it's second only to the line "You sure do sound a lot taller on the radio."

The truth is that getting to travel around the U.S. has been an incredible experience. Sharing stories from the road to readers online, listeners on-air, and viewers who see video segments about interesting people and places, is absolutely a great gig if you can get it.

The "dream job" is only a dream because of the people I get to meet along the way, and all of the experiences most people aren't fortunate enough to have—all in one lifetime. Travel isn't cheap, and time isn't endless. In the course of a year, I'm able to do things that most people won't be able to accomplish during their entire lifetimes. There's not a day on the road that goes by where I don't feel fortunate that I'm not sitting in a cubicle or digging a ditch along some country road.

Is covering travel important? I used to believe it wasn't. But as my audience has grown over the years, my attitude has changed. At least a bit. I hear from all sorts of people, from all different walks of life. Travel isn't political, and it shouldn't really be controversial either. Travel is something that brings people together. It also reminds you that not everyone has the means, or the ability, to do it.

One day I read an e-mail from a man who told me he found my website and reads it once a week. He explained that he was a wheelchair-bound military veteran and barely scraping by in his older years. He mentioned that he can't afford to travel, and even if he could, it would be a huge undertaking as he was single with no immediate family.

He went on to tell me I had become his window to the world and that he absolutely loves traveling across America through my stories and photos. I've received similar messages from people who don't get to travel but use my stories or videos as an escape in the middle of the day. As the years went by, the notes started coming in from beyond my home base of St. Louis, and even beyond our shores. It's still mind-boggling to me when I hear from people in places like Australia, Italy, or Brazil.

A gentleman from Canada recently sent me a note to tell me he had planned a month-long road trip with his son across the U.S. based on things he'd learned from my website. One of my favorite compliments came from a woman who bought a copy of *100 Things to Do in America Before You Die*. She told me that her family went through the entire book on Mother's Day and together, as a group, discussed previous family vacations, trips, and places, as well as those they all still wanted to take and see. She said it was the best Mother's Day she'd ever had. That was really touching.

Early on in my career covering travel, my dad would often tell people, "Bill's on vacation again." He wasn't being mean, or trying to diminish my work—he'd just see the fun pictures online and hear my phone updates when I called him from the car. Eventually, it got to the point where I decided to take him on a trip with me so he could see what I do. After about five hours into the first day he stopped, a bit short of breath, and said, "Man. How do you do this?"

I responded with: "How do I do what? *Vacation*?"

He hasn't told anyone I'm vacationing since.

It's true that trips can be long, and your schedule is usually

full. As time has gone on, I've learned two important rules for travel: always order water at meals (because you never get enough when you're on the road) and always get your rest. Most of us who cover travel are loaded up with things to see and do in different destinations.

People always ask the same questions when you tell them what you do for a living. The first question is always, "Who do you write for?" Sadly, I've yet to come up with a fast, easy-to-digest response. Truth is, almost no one writes for just one place these days. If you're reading an article in a newspaper or magazine, the author is most likely a freelance employee who pitched the story and writes for a dozen different outlets.

In order to survive, you have to wear a lot of hats, and learn how to juggle. For example, this week I've written pages for this book, several blog postings about a recent trip to Michigan, seven radio broadcasts about travel, two video segments for social media, and set up speaking appearances and worked on a newsletter that I send out once a month. I also don't leave work at 5:00 P.M. (However, I do get to stay home when it snows.)

The other question I get is, "How do you get paid?" I used to think that was sort of a rude question for people to ask, but I came to understand that people are just genuinely curious. In a nutshell, it takes a series of sponsors, freelance jobs, and random gigs to keep the lights on at my house.

Sadly, most media outlets don't want to pay for stories, or pay very little. People ask you to do things for free all of the time. Recently, a major publication that everyone knows reached out to me about using a photograph I took. Their fee for using my work? "Yeah, we'll give you a credit in the magazine," the woman offered. "Oh great," I responded. "I'm sure Bank of America will gladly accept your magazine credit as part of my mortgage payment."

Writers in general are rarely wealthy. If I had to guess, 95 percent of all book authors are not making six figures annually. And a significant number of them earn less than $10,000 a year from writing alone. All the more reason to support your favorite writers, and buy their books if you have the chance. I'm most thankful that I have a handful of different ways to make a living.

And the last of the most-asked questions is, "Where is the best place you've visited?" For this one, I just smile and decline to answer. The truth is: I don't have a single favorite place to visit. I've learned to find something positive in every place I travel to, which is easy to do if you make the effort. Of course, I'd be lying if I didn't admit that I have a few favorite small towns I like spending time in, and a handful of big cities I love to explore. But the honest-to-God truth is that I love being anywhere I can meet interesting people and can find at least one good story to share.

This book is full of good stories, funny moments, and unique experiences. I've tried to keep things light, but on a few occasions, I share some candid feelings about what I've learned on this wild adventure. Thanks for buying my book and helping to keep the gas tank full.

If you don't mind buying a second copy: I also need some new socks.

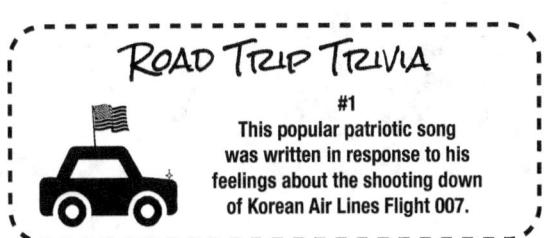

ROAD TRIP TRIVIA

#1
This popular patriotic song was written in response to his feelings about the shooting down of Korean Air Lines Flight 007.

MORE TO EXPLORE...
Visit the Indianapolis Motor Speedway that can seat 300,000 people!

Posing for a photo in Indianapolis with Olympic star Gabby Douglas.

IT'S A SMALL COUNTRY AFTER ALL

Traveling solo is something many Americans are not that fond of. However, I always suggest that everyone experience a weeklong road trip on their own, at least once. Not only do you get to pick the radio station you want to listen to without your friend or spouse constantly flipping the channel, you'll experience things you would have otherwise missed.

One of those experiences is talking to strangers. Getting to meet and learn about people in different parts of the country is one of my favorite parts of writing about travel and tourism.

One late fall afternoon in 2014, I was exploring Panama City Beach, Florida. PCB is best known as a "spring break" getaway, though it's a beautiful destination year-round, with 27 miles of beachfront. The beach, with its signature sugar-like sand, is nestled between two terrific state parks: St. Andrews and Camp Helen.

Camp Helen State Park, like many parks across the country, relies on volunteers to help with various programs or even simple tasks like cleaning up trash or greeting visitors at a welcome center. I had the chance to visit with one of these volunteers shortly after I arrived.

After exchanging a few pleasantries, the gentleman asked me what city or state I called home. I told him that I was from Missouri. The man smiled and said, "That's great! I'm also from Missouri. I live down here during the winter months." I responded by asking him where he lived in the state, and he said, "I live in the St. Louis area."

At this point, I was a bit shocked because St. Louis is also my hometown. However, it's amazing how many connections to STL I find when I travel. It's sort of a game I play—because on every single trip, it never fails—I will always meet someone who worked in, dated someone from, or was born in St. Louis.

I continued with the interrogation by asking, "Which part of St. Louis?" If you've never been there, it's an interesting combination of about 100 municipalities that make up the County. Then, of course, the city itself, which has a much smaller population—but it's where you'll find the Gateway Arch or Busch Stadium.

The gentleman answered my question and left me completely stunned when he named the very community that I currently call home, which has about 12,000 residents. Of course, this led to all sorts of discussions about local topics, including the future of a defunct mall that had recently been destroyed as well as some other small-town gossip and musings.

Out of curiosity, I asked the man what neighborhood his house was located in. He lived in the same subdivision! "This is unbelievable," I thought to myself, and at this point, my tour guide and some of the staff nearby were really getting a kick out of this wild, off-chance connection.

It turns out that the man I met by chance for the first time in Panama City Beach, Florida, lived in the house directly behind me.

I guess you could say: "It's a small country, after all."

THE THRIFTY BARBER

There was once a time when the greatest bastion of manhood was visiting the local barber shop for a fresh haircut or shave. As a child, you went with your dad and at a certain age, you made that trip on your own, officially as a grown man.

In Tunica, Mississippi, I learned about their long-time barber and beloved local citizen, Griff Lane. Lane's Barber Shop opened for business in 1928. Until his retirement in 1984, Mr. Lane gave haircuts for one dollar. After he was finished, he sprinkled sweet-smelling powder on the back of your neck and sent you off with a fresh piece of bubblegum.

Griff was the unofficial Tunica historian and archivist, even keeping track of the birthday of each citizen. He would call you on your birthday right at 7:00 A.M. "Good morning, happy birthday, happy birthday, and have a good day," was his standard line, according to Richard Taylor, who now runs the local Tunica History Museum.

Griff Lane was not only a beloved member of the community; he was also one of the most frugal people you'd ever meet. Hanging on the wall inside his barber shop was an electric clock, which he had received as a gift from a car dealership in town. Mr. Lane opened his shop every day at 6:00 A.M., closing each day at 6:00 P.M. At the end of each day, he unplugged the clock. The next business day, he'd open the shop, turn on the lights, and—right at 6:00 A.M.—he'd plug the clock back in.

In this part of the country, many people are die-hard fans of the St. Louis Cardinals baseball team. Mr. Lane was no exception and would talk baseball, good times and bad—with all of his customers and friends. One summer, a small group of guys decided they were going to make the trek to St. Louis and watch a game in person at the stadium. They left early one morning, and had made it all the way to the state line when Griff announced to his fellow passengers that they needed to turn around and go back to town.

Once back in Tunica, Griff informed the guys that he had forgotten to unplug the barber shop clock and didn't want to pay for electricity to power the clock for the two days he'd be out of town.

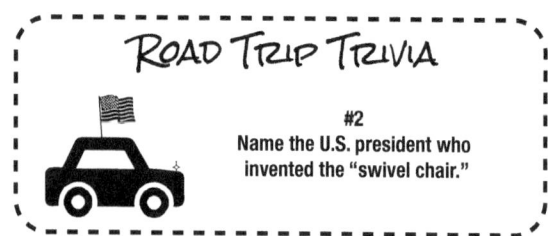

Road Trip Trivia

#2
Name the U.S. president who invented the "swivel chair."

A MUSEUM FOR EVERYTHING

There are about 40,000 museums in the United States and I feel like I've seen at least half of them. Some are massive in both size and the depth of their collections, like the National Civil Rights Museum in Memphis or the National World War II Museum in New Orleans. Others are modest, or even tiny, with only enough artifacts to fill a small room. The themes are just as wide-ranging as the sizes, with museums dedicated to foods, cars, companies, toys, music, celebrities, art, clothes, movies, history, sports, and even things like farm equipment, purses, bobbleheads, hair, or elevators.

These collections all serve a purpose, no matter how bizarre, boring, or ridiculous some of them may appear. I've always tried to come away with at least one interesting story or amusing bit of knowledge when I tour a new museum. Sometimes that's not possible. Sometimes you just laugh.

Take for example a trip through Springfield, Missouri, where a friend noted, "I think there's a hearing aid museum down the street." Sure enough, in a small building that used to be someone's house, two bedrooms were packed with nothing but hearing aid memorabilia. There were early models, a testing station, even manuals that instructed users on how to properly trim their ear hair.

In Middleton, Wisconsin, I visited the National Mustard Museum, which includes more than 6,000 varieties of mustard. The founder began his collection after a traumatic personal experience in 1986. His beloved Boston Red Sox had lost the World Series and he found himself in a 24-hour supermarket late in the evening, depressed from his team's disappointing finish. He decided to start collecting something to ease his mind, and, for whatever reason, he landed in the mustard section of the store. The museum's founder, a man named Barry Levenson, is the former assistant attorney general for the state of Wisconsin. He actually carried one of his beloved mustard tins in his pocket while arguing a case before the U.S. Supreme Court. He was quick to point out, "I won."

Early on, I was very cynical about the people who amass these bizarre collections. What I discovered is that most of them are actually pretty interesting people, and almost always have some sort of intriguing tale about how they began.

A few miles outside of Gettysburg, you can find a massive collection of more than 12,000 elephant-themed items. Dozens of billboards around town promote Mister Ed's Elephant Museum & Candy Emporium, which is a short drive from the historic battlefield. Ed Gotwalt ("Mr. Ed") began his collection after his sister-in-law gave him an elephant as a wedding gift many years ago.

"What am I supposed to do with this?" was his initial response to the bizarre present. "She told me it was for good luck," said Gotwalt. As time went on, his collection grew. Friends and co-workers would bring back elephant toys or jewelry from trips, while random strangers started sending their own elephant items to him. The most bizarre thing in the collection? An elephant hair dryer. His favorite piece was an elephant ring and necklace his wife purchased for his sixtieth birthday. During our interview, he was humble and thankful, often saying, "Everything in my life has been good."

Over time, I've gone from rolling my eyes to actively seeking out these people who hoard things for one reason or another. I've been to a museum full of vacuum cleaners in Missouri, and one in Kansas full of personal artifacts from motorcycle daredevil Evel Knievel. That collection included uniforms, bikes, board games, and even x-rays from his post-crash hospital visits. Some such collections are just downright bizarre, including one near San Antonio highlighting a bunch of painted toilet seat lids.

While the quirky collections make for fun stops along the way, there are many museums in the U.S. that could be classified as life-changing. For example, the Center For Puppetry Arts in Atlanta houses some of the most well-known puppets in American history. Seeing some of these pieces up close can take you back to childhood in a heartbeat. The museum was gifted a 500-piece Jim Henson collection that includes beloved characters from *Sesame Street* and *The Muppet Show*.

Kermit the Frog happened to be my first inspiration for performing and being on stage. Seeing the puppet up close was a special moment. The other characters on display include Bert and Ernie, Elmo, and many other Henson classics including Miss Piggy and Oscar the Grouch. The museum staff noted that it's not that strange to find guests crying as they see these characters in real life for the first time. They also shared the most amusing line heard in the gallery is apparently, "Wow. That's a big bird."

The National Museum of Play in Rochester, New York, brings up similar childhood memories as so many toys are on display that are relatable to any age group, whether it's the first talking baby doll (which looks incredibly frightening) or the first version of the Monopoly board, which is shaped in a circle. The National Museum of Toys & Miniatures in Kansas City is another favorite, featuring a large collection of fine-scaled miniatures.

On several occasions, I've had the good fortune to tour down below or behind these buildings into highly secured storage areas where most of those collections are kept. It's always a treat to have that opportunity because you realize how important museums are in preserving our history. For most

MORE TO EXPLORE...

At the Tabasco World Headquarters on Avery Island, Louisiana. The scenic driving tour is also a must.

large museums, only about 5 to 10 percent of all the items they own are out on display at any given time. That gives places like the Rock and Roll Hall of Fame in Cleveland, or The National Baseball Hall of Fame and Museum in Cooperstown a chance to rotate in new objects, giving visitors a reason to return down the road.

Some museums do have most of their important items out, as they tell a complete story about a particular topic or person. The Ringling in Sarasota, Florida, tells the story of the circus. The George Jones Museum in Nashville has all of the artifacts from the country music legend's personal life right down to his Costco membership card. Former president Jimmy Carter displays most of his personal things in Atlanta at his presidential museum. You'll see his Grammy award, passport, and even the sweater he wore on television while giving a famous speech on saving energy.

There are currently 13 official presidential museums that are run by the U.S. National Archives. Of course, there are others like the Abraham Lincoln Presidential Library and Museum in Springfield, that are run by a state government or a private organization. These museums are the single greatest American history lesson you can give yourself or a child. They are full of stories and actual items relating to the respective administrations that are one of a kind and priceless.

The George W. Bush Presidential Library and Museum displays the bullhorn used in New York City after 9-11, while the president stood on a pile of rubble and talked to emergency workers. President Johnson's museum—the LBJ Presidential Library—in Austin has the table on which the Civil Rights Act was signed. There are so many pieces of history, from Oval Office telephones to scripts used for historic speeches that impacted our way of life.

World of Coca-Cola, one of the most interactive and complete museum collections, tells the story of a major American brand. The number of Coke-related artifacts on display is nothing short of incredible. Every bottle, lunch box, T-shirt, or poster ever made seems to be featured. They also feature thoughtful exhibits like a taste testing station that lets you sample every product they ship around the world. The Dr Pepper Museum and Free Enterprise Institute, while smaller than its Coca-Cola counterpart, is actually located inside the company's first bottling plant, in Waco, Texas. You can still see the artesian well that was used producing the early bottles of soda.

I'd regret not mentioning that there are also plenty of museums in America that are just downright creepy. Most of these aren't museums in the traditional sense, but rather buildings that have some sort of collection or historic purpose. Near the top of the list is the Glore Psychiatric Museum in St. Joseph, Missouri, which used to be a hospital. It's no longer a working hospital, but visitors can walk through the building and admire eerie-looking devices once used to treat patients, like something known as "the lunatic box."

Of course, there are lots of sports-related museums. College basketball, the NFL, even NASCAR, which has a museum where you can do a virtual ride in a race car and time yourself to see how long it takes to change a set of tires.

Sometimes, the best museums to explore are the ones where you have absolutely no concept or interest in the subject matter. For example, Oklahoma City is home to the American Banjo Museum. Going in, I was completely ignorant about the fascinating history of the instrument, and I certainly didn't have any real appreciation for the wide variety of styles that are available. That changed after a visit to the museum in the city's Bricktown district.

Museums of all sizes and topics are an important part of telling the American story. Experience as many of them as you can. I'm constantly surprised at how much I've learned.

For example, I've now seen enough music-related exhibits to know that if you want to have a hit song, your odds certainly increase if you write your original lyrics on a napkin or hotel note pad.

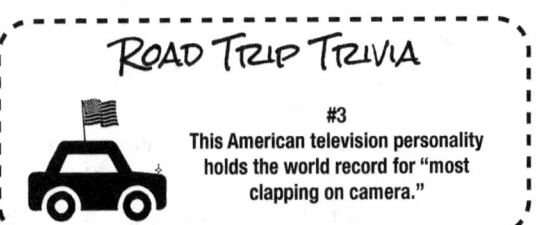

ROAD TRIP TRIVIA

#3
This American television personality holds the world record for "most clapping on camera."

FIRE IN THE HOLE

Traveling alone is not something most people are comfortable with. Having a road trip companion is great, but you often miss out on a lot of opportunities and learning experiences. Being on your own allows you to completely focus on things you may miss if you're on a journey with a loved one or friend. One of the things I really enjoy about traveling solo is that I'm forced to meet new people and open my eyes to all walks of life. One comment I hear frequently is, "It must be lonely out on the road." But the reality is that I'm probably lonelier at home.

Making new friends has been a favorite part of traveling across America. I often joke that I'll continue this line of work until I have a free place to stay in every city in the country. And I'm getting pretty close.

A couple of years ago, I stayed with friends in Mississippi while on a book tour through the South. There are several states that have unfortunate stereotypes that will never go away. Mississippi is one of them. Yes, there are pockets of poverty and folks who never quite got over the loss of the Civil War. However, to dismiss the entire state and the majority of its residents because of a small number of rednecks who always manage to get their faces on the news is a mistake. I've met some incredible people in this state and have returned numerous times—on purpose.

That's not to say that on occasion, I start to doubt myself. Driving to my friend's property, which sits way out in the country, I approached a pick-up truck driving on the wrong side of the road. Slowing down, focusing hard on the scene in front of me, I saw a man pointing a long shotgun out of his window, taking aim, and then firing at birds hovering over a field.

At this point, I switched gears from curious traveler to frightened driver. I sped up, zoomed frantically into the opposite lane of traffic, and passed by the rusty blue pick-up truck, inside of which a shirtless man in overalls was staring me down.

On a completely different visit to the same friend's house, I was told they had a surprise waiting for me. The friends, who shall remain nameless, are two of the loveliest people you'd ever want to meet. They are generous, intelligent, and despite the familiar Mississippi drawl, do not fit into the classic Deep South stereotype. They do live far from any big towns, and have a beautiful farm complete with a decent-sized lake.

At some point early on in our friendship, they had mentioned that one of their neighbors had perfected some sort of a science project while studying YouTube videos. Essentially, the neighbor had built his own homemade cannon. Always curious, I must have mentioned that this was something I'd like to see—because that turned out to be the big surprise waiting for me.

The neighbor and his girlfriend joined us for dinner on the farm. He was a stocky gentleman, about six feet tall, displaying two brand-new cigars resting in the pocket of his light gray T-shirt. He had a gray mustache, brown baseball hat, and discolored teeth. She was an older woman from Mexico, wearing a bright yellow dress, barely speaking any English. As I watched their back and forth conversations, I actually wondered if perhaps she was being held hostage. Unfortunately, I didn't know how to say, "Blink twice if you need me to call the cops" in Spanish.

Dinner was uncomfortable—the man had dubious opinions on pretty much everything. As though on cue, the foreign girlfriend mumbled something nobody at the table understood at the end of each of his statements. He didn't even like Willie Nelson. Who doesn't like Willie Nelson?

After dinner concluded, we headed outside for the big reveal. There on the lawn, having been unloaded from a trailer and wheeled into the back yard, was a homemade cannon. It looked like a large, rusty propane canister with one end sawn off. It was propped up by a metal rod that allowed it to be aimed low to the ground or straight into the air.

Too good not to document on film, this is the exact transcript of my brief interview with the man. For the sake of protecting his identity, we'll just call him "Bob."

> Bill: "So, sir, you said your name was Bob?"
> Bob: "Yep. Bob."
> Bill: "And Bob, you discovered on YouTube how to make a cannon?"
> Bob: "Yep."
> Bill: "You should only do this out in the country, right?"
> Bob: "Yep."
> Bill: "And, I understand, inside the cannon is a bowling ball?"
> Bob: "Yep."
> Bill: "And the bowling ball is going to go how far?"
> Bob: "Probably about 400 yards down range."
> Bill: "So it's going to fly over the lake."
> Bob: "Yep."
> Bill: "I don't think I've ever seen a cannon this close before— I assume there will be a big boom?"
> Bob: "Yep."

Okay, well, thanks for the enlightening interview, Bob.

He then starts to light a fuse that is at least four feet long and explains, "If you look directly at the cannon, you'll never see the ball." I'm thinking to myself, "Is there even really a damn ball in there?" The entire thing started to seem like a bad idea. My video was destined to either make it to *America's Funniest Home Videos*, or on a constant loop at my funeral showing my loved ones how I tragically left planet Earth.

"Fire in the hole," Bob announces, as though he had just woken up from a nap. It was like listening to the Kentucky Derby and the announcer yawning while he says, "And down the stretch they come." At this point, the abducted Mexican girlfriend mumbles something from the patio about her iPad. Bob then screams over, "Yeah, it's about ready to go. Are you getting it?"

In the background of my video, you can hear nervous laughter and see the camera start to shake as I move back farther from the launch site. "VERY SOON!," Bob angrily yells over in response to something the girlfriend asks. Oh sure, now he's excited.

And then it happens. A ball of fire erupts from the cannon and BOOM! A cloud of dust hides the homemade device from view and somewhere in the sky, floating over the lake and into the woods, is the bowling ball. I never did see the ball, but could hear it whistling across the sky, I assume due to the three holes drilled on top.

"It's coming down," Bob informs us. Nobody can see anything. Everyone is coughing from the smoke. Bob confidently concludes: "It's in the woods."

God, I love Mississippi.

MORE TO EXPLORE...
The first Pizza Hut is now a museum on the campus of Wichita State University.

A MILLION-DOLLAR ROOF

Wichita, Kansas, is known for launching quite a few successful businesses. Perhaps the most notable is the worldwide restaurant chain Pizza Hut. The very first store location is now a museum, located on the campus of Wichita State University.

In the summer of 1958, Dan and Frank Carney opened a small pizza shop with the help of a $600 loan from their mother. The museum is small, but the location is fitting considering it's now part of Wichita State's "innovation campus." The brick building, also known as "store #1," serves as an inspiration to students with big ideas and dreams of their own.

Inside the Original Pizza Hut Museum are several video presentations that feature personal stories from the Carney brothers about opening their first location. Another video features a former CEO talking about the growing pains of the company, while another video plays the first Pizza Hut commercial jingle.

As for memories of starting the first Pizza Hut location in Wichita—Dan Carney vividly recalls how opening night went: "It was absolute chaos."

For me, the most interesting story told in the museum is how the franchise stores got their iconic "hut"-shaped roofing. The Carney brothers had found success in their pizza restaurants but they weren't exactly "rolling in dough," if you'll forgive the pun. In 1969, as the chain continued to expand, Pizza Hut wanted all its stores to look the same. They hired a Wichita artist named Richard Burke. Mr. Burke's fee of $30,000 to design the buildings proved too steep for the company.

A counter offer of $100 for each new location opened was agreed upon.

The final design was the now-iconic, instantly recognizable, 1950's-style red roof. That roof, which has its own patent, was incorporated into the company's logo in 1971.

Mr. Burke, even in his wildest dreams, could never have imagined that Pizza Hut would go on to open more than 17,000 locations around the world. By not walking away when the Carneys couldn't afford his initial fee, he wound up earning over $1,000,000.

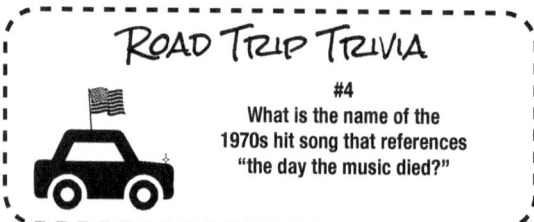

ROAD TRIP TRIVIA

#4
What is the name of the 1970s hit song that references "the day the music died?"

COOPERSTOWN

Watching my dad peek into Stan Musial's locker at the National Baseball Hall of Fame seemed to bring our family's baseball story full circle.

"My father always wanted to leave early," Dad said, remembering. He's now 67; his first game was back in 1958. "Plus, we sat in right field at Sportsman's Park where there was a fence and no chance to ever catch anything. I always wanted to go to left field where Musial would throw balls into the stands. But your grandpa made me sit there because it had easy access to get out and beat the traffic."

I've been a huge baseball fan my entire life, which probably makes sense for a kid who grew up in St. Louis. Perhaps it was watching Ozzie Smith do back-flips when the Cardinals took the field. Perhaps it was getting to stay up past my bedtime until Jack Buck finally said the words, "That's a winner." Or perhaps it was going to Busch Stadium with my dad and learning what truly makes baseball America's favorite pastime.

My baseball story is probably a lot like yours. Dad introduced us to the game of baseball. We played catch, collected cards, and went to as many games as we could afford. Sound familiar? Probably, although odds are your father parked a lot closer.

We were dirt poor—though, to be honest, we didn't really know it at the time. My parents had divorced and Dad worked in a warehouse, shipping boxes of air conditioning valves. Like many other single parents who magically find ways to stretch a dollar, our dad made certain that we experienced Cardinal baseball early on. Our first taste of baseball heaven came in the mid-'80s. Bleacher seats were two dollars. On days when there was a giveaway, we'd get there early. Hot dogs? Nachos? Nope.

Our stadium snacks consisted of Kool-Aid in a Tupperware mug and a plastic bag of plain-label peanuts and pretzels that we brought with us.

"I told you boys that you had to be well-behaved or we wouldn't go back," Dad recalls. "You and your brother didn't ask for anything. Even total strangers in the bleachers would comment on how well-behaved you both were." It's impossible to recall your mindset at seven years old, but clearly we understood that the focus of a trip to the stadium wasn't to run around, or beg for an overpriced foam finger or cotton candy—it was to soak in this magical game of baseball. We learned the rules, always came equipped with a glove to catch a foul ball, and, for God's sake, didn't even dream about leaving before the last out of the last inning.

In the picture-perfect setting of fall in Cooperstown, New York, we stepped foot into a place where fathers and sons have been sharing sweet memories for decades. I'd certainly love to believe that only in Cardinal Nation do we get to cherish that special baseball bond, but it absolutely transcends teams, cities, and races. Yes, even Cubs fans.

One young boy posed for a picture in front of Babe Ruth's jersey while his father snapped the perfect shot with an iPhone. Another father and son duo—they were from Gettysburg, Pennsylvania—couldn't get up the stairs fast enough to see the memorabilia on display for their favorite team, the Baltimore Orioles. A gentleman from Detroit pushed his 80-year-old father from exhibit to exhibit in a wheelchair. "Hold on, Pop, I'm gonna push you in here for a nice picture," he said as he guided the chair into a mock-up of Hank Aaron's locker. They were Tiger fans and had made the drive all the way to upstate New York.

As we explored the museum, each item behind glass brought

With my dad at Doubleday Field in Cooperstown, New York.

up personal reflections of our baseball memories. A bat used by Mark McGwire to hit his seventieth home run, a helmet worn during the game in which Fernando Tatis hit two grand slams. A glove belonging to Ozzie Smith reminded us that my dad wanted to name my brother after the Hall of Fame shortstop. The Cardinals were playing game two of the 1982 World Series when he was born. Apparently "Ozzie Clevlen" was vetoed in favor of "Brian."

In the museum store, my dad spotted another Cardinal fan with a Bob Gibson jersey, which drummed up more childhood memories. "Gibson was my favorite!" he told the stranger. With a smile, the man replied, "Thank you, sir! Mine, too!"

As we ended our visit with a stop to Doubleday Field around the corner, a man from Philadelphia kindly took our photo sitting in the bleachers of the historic stadium. "You're smart to take this trip with your dad while you still can," the man said. "I wish I would have done the same thing when my dad was alive."

Asked if I was going to buy a T-shirt or a key chain to remember our visit to Cooperstown, I told my dad, "Nah, I don't need another T-shirt." The truth is: I won't need anything to remind me of our visit. I will absolutely never forget it.

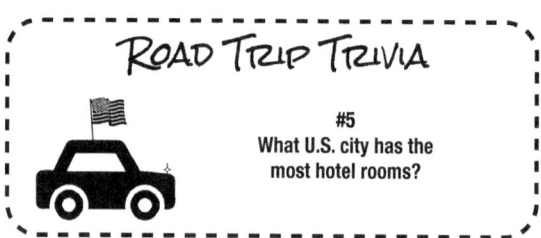

ROAD TRIP TRIVIA

#5
What U.S. city has the most hotel rooms?

TRICK OR TREAT

The occasional traveler enjoys the perks of staying in a hotel probably more than those of us that are frequently on the road. One of those perks are the tiny bottles of shampoo, bath gel, and lotion. And everyone has done the same trick—tossing all the bottles into your suitcase even if you don't use them, just to magically see brand-new bottles appear on the bathroom counter top the next day.

When I first started traveling, with zero shame, I took every single item that was laid out by the hotel staff. By the end of the first year, I had amassed an embarrassing amount of those complimentary products. While at home, I never had to worry about buying anything bathroom related. I had baskets full of anything you'd need— soap, shampoo, tissues, even sewing kits. All stuffed into plastic baskets in my closet.

Several years ago, I was returning home from a trip and making my way through the neighborhood when I realized that it was Halloween.

It was still light out and only a handful of kids were walking around, but I knew it was too late to go and get a bag of candy. So I sat in the car for a few minutes, pondering some sort of a solution. And then it hit me.

Under the kitchen sink I had an orange metal container, complete with the Jack-O-Lantern face, that someone had given to me years ago. I cleaned it out, walked back to my bathroom, and filled it to the brim with tiny bottles of shampoo, bath gels, and conditioner.

It was the cleanest Halloween my subdivision has ever seen.

DUDE...SLOW DOWN!

I've been lucky during my lifetime to have a lot of those "pinch yourself" moments where you have to stop, take a deep breath, and say aloud: "Am I really standing here?" One of those times was on the lawn of the White House in Washington, DC.

If you're fortunate enough to visit what is easily the most recognized home in the world, you'll probably go through a similar experience. Obviously, there are multiple layers of security and, depending on the nature of your visit, you'll already have been put through a background check by the FBI.

Once you go through various checkpoints and a final x-ray machine for your personal belongings, chances are you'll be standing on the driveway, just beyond the doors of the east wing of the building. From this vantage point, the front gate looks so far away. You can see a mob of tourists taking photos, alongside various protesters with signs, though you can't really hear any of them. You certainly can't read the signs.

This was the moment I stopped and took it all in, knowing nearly every person on the planet at some point has thought about being a visitor at the White House.

Once you walk through the doors of the East Wing, the first thing you notice are the paintings. Each president and first lady have an official portrait and many of them are hanging in what amounts to a lobby area once you step inside. While the paintings are certainly nice, I can't honestly say I had much interest in wasting my limited time in the White House giving each portrait a once-over.

Clearly sensing my lack of interest, and noting the acceleration of my pace, a Secret Service agent stepped in my direction and shouted, "Hey, slow down!" Immediately, I froze and wondered if I was going to be kicked out after only walking in the door just two minutes earlier. The agent, a stocky man in his early thirties, started to grin with both palms up in the air, shrugging his shoulders. He said, "Dude…slow down, you're in the White House."

Of course, his point was immediately taken—and he was right. It may be a while, maybe never, that I'll have the chance to soak up being here and I needed to savor each moment—even if it meant admiring a full-body portrait of Hillary Clinton in a blue pantsuit.

Once you start moving toward the middle of the White House, you go down a hallway with windows that show the South Lawn. Out on the lawn, a staff member was playing with the Obama's dog. It was a week or two before Thanksgiving, so holiday decorations were starting to be installed.

There are several rooms that are typically viewable by the public. You can see the Library, China Room, Blue Room, Red Room, and a few others on the main floor. You'll probably see the State Dining Room, where those fancy VIP functions are typically held, and you'll have a chance to see the East Room, which is where a lot of press conferences and historic speeches to the nation have taken place. You'll note the red carpet, most likely rolled up at the end of the hall where you've seen presidents walk down toward the podium.

You tend to forget how old the building is, and—while it's technically a mansion—it's really more of a museum that people live and work in. It is not as glamorous as you'd imagine, and, in a way, that makes it sort of special. If you ever have the chance to visit, learn from my experience. Walk slowly and soak it all up. Even the boring portraits.

COME ON DOWN

Being a member of *The Price Is Right* audience is a popular bucket list item many travelers try to check off when they visit southern California. For most of us, the daytime TV game show was a part of our childhood and something we enjoyed on those rare days we were able to stay home from school. Others love to watch during their lunch hour at the office. No matter where you've seen the program—everyone at some point dreams about hearing their name, followed by: "Come on down!"

I was fortunate enough to see one of the last episodes that TV legend Bob Barker hosted, shortly before he retired. As a bit of a production geek, I was far more interested in the behind-the-scenes activity than I was in the cost of a brand-new microwave oven or kitchen set.

The studio is located at the CBS Television City complex in Los Angeles. It is a massive piece of real estate that has been home to many well-known shows over the years. From soap operas, to sitcoms and TV specials, the halls are full of history. One thing that's interesting is that while TPIR is taping, none of the other nearby studios are in use because it's so loud. (I mean, how awkward would it be to film a love scene on *The Young and The Restless* and hear the sound of people cheering in the background?)

The studio itself is pretty small and much more intimate than it seems on television. Even before you enter the building, producers have already scoped out who they want on stage, through interviews and eavesdropping as you stand in line. As you watch the show at home, you hear the announcer tell contestants to "Come on down." However, in the audience, you don't hear that. Instead, you see a guy holding a cue card off to the side of the stage, with names written in large letters.

Winning on the show is probably not worth the hassle of paying taxes and trying to find someone to buy the items you really didn't want in the first place. But being part of the audience is certainly a fun experience.

After the show concluded and the rest of the audience made their way to the exit, I walked over to a random gentleman leaning against the stage and introduced myself. Obviously, he had no idea who I was but he took an interest and we began a conversation about the TV business and broadcasting in general. It turned out that he was in charge of managing the studios for the entire complex and as I was set to walk away, he asked, "Would you like a backstage tour?"

Trying to remain cool, I said something to the effect of "Oh, sure, I guess—if you have the time." Truth be told, it was absolutely thrilling and a real eye-opener, even though I was pretty familiar with the industry. He took pictures of me coming through the curtains, standing in the contestant's row, and even making myself at home on the Showcase Showdown platform. I saw the directors' booth and many of the popular games we've all loved—including the famous Plinko board just propped up, lifeless, against the wall.

We walked onto all of the sets that were open in each studio, and took a look at the department where props were built, including new games that were set to make an appearance on *The Price Is Right*. We went up to the private helicopter landing pad where the CBS executives would jet off for meetings, with a great view of the Hollywood sign from the roof.

For whatever reason, my most vivid memory is nearly tripping over something in the middle of the hallway on my way to the parking lot. A quick glance down revealed the prize wheel from *Wheel of Fortune* just sitting on the floor, about to be re-painted.

INTERNATIONAL HERO

There's a great scene in *National Lampoon's Vacation* where Chevy Chase's character, "Clark," has just robbed a cash register and stops for a quick glance at the Grand Canyon with his wife and kids. That scene, which was filmed on location, is what many people seem to do when they make the trip to one of America's most popular national parks. In fact, some figures suggest that less than five percent of all visitors experience the Canyon below the rim.

My first visit to the Grand Canyon was in March of 2015. It was covered in snow and the hiking paths were still icy. On this particular trip, I was with a group of other travel writers and bloggers and, sadly, hiking was not part of the agenda. Looking back, I am thankful that I spoke up and made the decision to break away from the group and its scheduled plans and went hiking.

Joining me was a travel writer from Colorado who was an experienced hiker and used to the changes in altitude that can be tricky on those of us from the Midwest. We geared up: boots, walking sticks, and clamp-ons that attach to the bottom of your boots for extra traction. You can never be too prepared when hiking the Grand Canyon, especially in the winter months. After all … one slip in the wrong place, and it's lights out for good.

Unlike my colleague, I was not an experienced hiker. I'm in pretty good shape, not overweight or afraid to walk long distances. But about two miles down, I decided that I'd had enough. We stopped at a common photo stop called Ooh-Ahh-Point along the South Kaibab Trail. It's this spot that made me especially glad that I made the effort to really experience

MORE TO EXPLORE...

Winter is the best time to visit the Grand Canyon, with fewer tourists than the warmer months.

the Grand Canyon. What you see from the parking lot or an overlook is nothing compared to what it's like once you're actually down inside.

My hiking partner decided to keep going because she really knew what she was doing, but I decided to head back up. Before starting on my return journey, I noticed two young ladies posing for photos on one of the rocks. They were doing what so many (mostly younger) people do: Pushing the limits of safety in order to get a great picture.

Clearly, I had no authority to tell anyone what to do in a national park or anywhere else for that matter—but I did speak up. "Excuse me, would you girls not do that?" I yelled. They looked over as I added, "That's really dangerous. It would be awful if you slipped and fell."

They were both 18 years old and visiting the United States from Germany. Who knows—maybe they were under the impression I was an undercover park ranger. Regardless, they did listen to my advice and came down from the large rock. I approached them and said, "Thank you. I didn't want to see anything happen to you." Of course, what I was really thinking was: "I didn't want to have to fill out a bunch of paperwork if I witnessed you falling."

We chatted for a bit and I learned that they were in the country for two months. They had finished school, saved up some money, and decided to explore. Pretty brave to visit another country on your own at that age. They ticked off a long list of places they had already been, which was impressive. At eighteen, I hadn't started exploring my own neighborhood, let alone a new country across the ocean. I managed to interview them briefly on my recorder so my radio audience could hear about our meeting.

At some point, I glanced down and noticed something

that struck me as odd. Both of the girls were wearing slip-on, lightweight shoes that you'd use for a day at the beach. I have no idea how on earth they had made it down that far, how they didn't slide off the edge of the trail, or how they managed to not fall off the giant rock.

One thing was for certain: there was no way these two girls were going to make it out of there in those shoes. They quickly realized the same thing as we all started to head back to the top.

After they spoke to each other in German, slipping and sliding, both with nervous looks on their faces, I said, "All right. Here's the deal. I've got traction on my boots, and two walking poles; you can hang on to me."

So off we went. For the next ninety minutes as I chipped away at ice and slowly walked uphill, both of these young German girls clung onto me. One on each arm. As tourists hiked down, going the opposite direction, it had to appear like an episode of the TV sitcom *Three's Company*.

I had to stop every ten minutes or so as my head felt like it was going to explode from the pressure. Even on this relatively easy hike, the altitude change can be brutal on your body. Each time I stopped for a quick rest and to catch my breath, the girls would speak to each other in German. "They better not be talking crap about me," I thought to myself.

We finally made it to the very top where both girls gave me a hug and thanked me. It was a learning experience for all of us. They learned the perils of wearing inappropriate shoes, and I learned not to look down at them.

THE CANDY MACHINE

On several occasions, I've toured the legendary Motown studios in Detroit, Michigan. Hitsville U.S.A. has been open to the public since the mid-1980s and is full of great stories.

It's essentially a two-story house that was transformed into an office and recording facility. The music label cranked out some of the best-known soul songs in history along with some of the biggest names in popular music. Smokey Robinson, The Temptations, Michael Jackson, Marvin Gaye, and so many other beloved artists and groups.

As you walk in through the front door, you notice a small desk where a young lady named Diana Ross used to answer the phone. An engineering room is visible just beyond the lobby through a glass window, which looks down onto the legendary Motown recording studio.

But it's at the end of the hall, just around the corner from the studio's soundproof door, that a vintage piece of Motown history rests, as thousands of visitors walk by each week, often unaware of its role in the Motown story.

In 1961, Stevie Wonder began his Motown career at the young age of 11. He became known as "Little Stevie Wonder" and had his first hit with "Fingertips, Part 2" in 1963. He could sing and play multiple instruments, and was known for his writing ability, making him a bit of an "old soul." Stevie became blind shortly after his premature birth. While his lack of sight never stopped him from achieving musical success, it did cause the occasional roadblock in other aspects of life.

A candy machine with five options for treats was available to everyone in the building. For a quarter, you would spin the knob that displayed the treat you desired, and it fell down into an opening below.

Stevie Wonder was known to love Baby Ruth candy bars. The problem was that he couldn't tell which of the slots had his favorite treat. After learning of the issue, the staff instructed the company that stocked the machine to always put Baby Ruth candy bars in the middle dispenser, so Stevie would always know they were there.

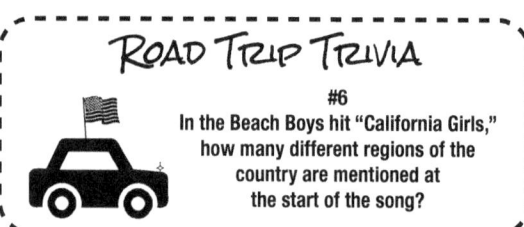

ROAD TRIP TRIVIA

#6
In the Beach Boys hit "California Girls," how many different regions of the country are mentioned at the start of the song?

GOATS ON THE ROOF

Door County, Wisconsin, is one of the most beautiful places in the Midwest, particularly in the summer months. From lake views to historic lighthouses, the entire region is an absolute treasure. Locals are friendly, there's plenty to do, and—if cherries are your thing—you're bound to get your fill.

Driving along Bay Shore Drive in Sister Bay, Wisconsin, you're sure to notice something that might seem a bit out of place. In fact, if it doesn't seem out of place…well, there may be something wrong with you. Al Johnson's Swedish Restaurant opened in 1949. It's a beloved hot spot—especially for breakfast—featuring their famous "square" Swedish pancakes.

But it's not the pancakes or those delicious lingonberries, nor the traditionally dressed Swedish employees, that make Al Johnson's stand out. It's the roof of their building, completely covered in grass with half a dozen goats to be seen grazing about during the day.

The quirky tradition started back in 1973 when one of Al's prankster pals arrived with a ladder and a goat. He climbed up top with the goat and left it there for Al to discover. From that day forward, Door County residents and tourists have seen goats on the roof of Al Johnson's Restaurant. They do not make an appearance if it's cold, windy, or rainy. They are not forced to get on the roof. In fact, each day it's the same routine: the goats get to choose if they want to hop into the truck that takes them to Sister Bay.

Other businesses around the country have tried to replicate the experience, but Al Johnson's was the first. In fact, the entire idea is trademarked.

On a recent visit to Door County, I was invited to climb up

on the iconic roof, an experience that made quite a few of my fellow travelers jealous. The goats were pretty laid back. (After all, they are known to listen to NPR when they're back at the Johnson family farm.) As the ducks and I convened up on the roof, tourists stopped in their tracks as they realized it was not an illusion or the after effect of too many Wisconsin brews. "Yes, those really are goats walking around, sleeping, or eating the grass on top of the building," I explained.

As dozens of people grabbed their phones to take photos, it wasn't clear if they wanted shots of the goats or if they were merely hoping to watch me fall off the roof.

MORE TO EXPLORE...
Get your fill of cherry products! More than 2,500 acres of cherries are in Door County.

On the famous roof of Al Johnson's Restaurant in Sister Bay, Wisconsin.

TRAGEDY AND HUMANITY

In 2016, I made a stop in the southern Missouri town of Joplin, nearly five years after a devastating tornado tore the town apart. Bringing it up in conversation brought visible emotions to each of the residents I met. One girl started crying as she recalled the gut-wrenching sounds outside her bathroom window as the storm blew through her neighborhood. Others spoke about strangers helping one another and the real sense of community that seems to surface after one of these tragedies. No matter who you talked with, it was obvious that this was still a town with a lot of healing left to do.

On May 22, 2011, one of the most destructive tornadoes in American history touched down, putting Joplin on the map in ways they never imagined or wanted.

At 5:34 P.M. on a Sunday afternoon, an EF5 tornado blew through the city best known for its ties to Route 66 or connections to Bonnie and Clyde, who appeared here during their infamous run from the law. (The first photo of Bonnie was discovered here.) But on this dark day, the world would learn of Joplin as a small community at the mercy of Mother Nature through no fault of its own.

One hundred sixty-one people lost their lives and more than 1,150 additional residents were injured. Entire city blocks were leveled. Even today, it's largely obvious where the tornado came through town—either through empty lots of land or new homes that seem slightly out of place.

There's a bizarre contrast between kids happily playing on slides and swings in a city park, just yards away from a memorial that features quotes from survivors and the names of all who died. It's impossible to read the first-hand accounts and not feel the emotion run through your body. Even in the midst of sadness, there's fresh optimism from those who survived.

One resident opined, "I have a new perspective on life now. Things that I used to be afraid of, I'm not afraid of anymore, and I can't explain it. I've never been happier in my life; I've never been more content."

If you've never lived in the Midwest, the threat of tornadoes can be frightening. Yet anyone who's routinely in the path of these storms knows we tend to be jaded by alarms and sirens and typically run to the front porch to look at the sky instead of heading to the basement like we should. Joplin residents were no different. But this storm was.

Melodee Colbert-Kean served as mayor of Joplin from 2012 to 2014. She remembers going outside to watch the action before she realized something was different. "I went outside to watch and noticed a tree in my front yard bending all the way to the ground. Then I heard a second siren go off. That's when I knew this storm was different than the others."

And it was.

A third of the city was destroyed as 200 miles per hour winds created three million cubic yards of residential debris. Over 7,500 city dwellings were affected or destroyed. More than 1,300 pets were displaced from their owners. This was a city thrust into complete chaos.

As we share recovery stories over a catfish lunch at her soul food restaurant, ME's Place, the former mayor talks about how so many people came together when it mattered most.

"When disaster happens, people band together. I don't know what it is but we band together to help our neighbors, something we should do on a daily basis, but we don't. Anybody you walked by—they were trying to help someone else."

Even five years after the tornado, people from all over the

world were coming to help Joplin. A beautiful map in City Hall artfully shows how many people have reached out to this community as volunteers, many of them immediately after the storm. Mrs. Kean noted that, "People from as far away from Japan and India showed up to help. That's what makes you believe in humanity."

I heard similar stories along the Mississippi Gulf Coast during the tenth anniversary of Hurricane Katrina. One woman talked about climbing into a tree to save her life, while another talked about feeling helpless as she watched everything that she owned float away. Despite the significant damage, there was a constant theme among survivors: there are still plenty of good people out there.

One of my favorite small towns in America has become Bay St. Louis, Mississippi. The first time I drove into downtown, I ventured over to their beautiful marina to take a look around. I noticed a young man, no older than fifteen, cutting up and cleaning a fish he had just caught off the deck. I asked him if this was something he did often and in a deep southern accent he replied, "Yes, sir." Turns out that, several times a week, this teenager catches and cooks his own dinner. That's not something you see in many parts of the country. I didn't even do my own laundry at age fifteen, let alone catch my own dinner.

There's a beautiful historic train depot in downtown Bay St. Louis that houses a couple of local museums. One of the volunteers shared her personal story with me, echoing the thoughts of others that were so thankful for the kindness and generosity of complete strangers. This tiny town took the first impact of the hurricane, and, while New Orleans had all of the media coverage, this was the place that was hit the hardest.

She told me that, one afternoon, while trying to clean her completely flooded home, a man in a truck parked in the street

MORE TO EXPLORE...
Visitors can enjoy 32 miles of beautiful sandy beaches in Gulf Shores and Orange Beach, Alabama.

Hanging out with a Eurasian lynx at the Alabama Gulf Coast Zoo.

and set up a barbecue pit in the middle of the road. She had no idea who he was, and she never saw him again. He came to make lunch for people, serving them hot dogs, hamburgers, chips, and drinks. No charge, just wanted to do something helpful. Tearing up, the woman asked, "Do you know how much that means when you don't have power or a place to sleep and someone just shows up to feed you lunch?"

Gulf Shores, Alabama, finds itself in the track of big storms more often than not. One of my favorite interviews was with local celebrity Patti Hall. There's not a person in town that doesn't recognize the name. And it didn't take but a few minutes to understand why people in this part of the state remember her, admire her, and maybe—just maybe—some think she might be just a bit off her rocker.

Of course, I say that with the utmost affection, as I found Ms. Hall to be one of the most interesting people I've met while covering travel. Sitting on a picnic table while watching baby kangaroos bounce around, we talked about everything from her background to her time in the spotlight as a national celebrity.

As director of the Alabama Gulf Coast Zoo, Patti Hall has no formal training in running a zoo. "When I was younger, I wanted to be a veterinarian. This will show my age, but back then, they didn't allow women into vet schools. So, what else was there to do but became an art major and a hippie?"

Always an animal lover, she came to volunteer at the small zoo, sometimes putting in 40 hours a week. Having worked with other not-for-profit organizations and with some background in business, Patti was the perfect fit when the zoo started running into financial trouble. Today, the zoo is self-sufficient, with reasonable admission fees, and is a favorite destination among tourists that come to town for spring break or summer vacations.

"I get more compliments from people who say they have never been to a zoo where they can actually be close enough to see the animals blink," says Hall.

Animal interactions are a big part of what makes this place a unique visitor experience. During my visit, I step into an enclosed shelter with several ruffed lemurs that crawl all over me. "She really likes you," proclaims Patti. Apparently, the female lemur napping on my shoulder doesn't get close to many visitors. Another interaction takes place with a baby sloth that had a face that only a mother could love. I feed the thing some grapes and pray it isn't going to rip my eyeballs out.

Patti shares, "There are certain times in an animal's life where it's perfectly safe for them to be exposed to humans like this. It's great to be able to let people get close and develop a real appreciation and respect for them."

Some are lucky enough to experience the animals even closer than do others. Patti coaxed me into walking through the security gate on several stops during our tour of the zoo. Our first stop is to see two tigers that she raised personally in her home from the time they were several months old. There's no doubt that they know exactly who she is. There's also no doubt they can both hear my heart about to beat out of my chest as I stand nearby, watching the interaction. I've never been this close to a creature so gigantic. They both respond to Patti's calls to come over and visit us. Scratching against the fence where we are standing, they make a noise known as "chuffing." She reaches through the fence and gently pets them while she tells me to come a little bit closer.

Yeah, whatever, lady.

There's a reason everyone in town knows the name Patti Hall. Not only did she turn around the Alabama Gulf Coast Zoo; she became an instant celebrity here and around the world in 2004 when Hurricane Ivan made landfall in Gulf Shores. The powerful storm forced the evacuation of residents in the region—and yes, that included zoo animals.

And where did they go? To Patti's house, of course. All 280 of them. Six tigers, two lions, cougars, bears, monkeys of all sizes, deer, goats, donkeys, and even her staff members' pets, along with their owners who also came to live on her property. The only thing left behind was an 11-foot-long alligator. It's certainly hard to fault anyone for that.

News crews in town covering the storm caught wind of the massive animal evacuation, and it instantly became a focus of national news networks and newspapers around the world. Sitting in her office, we watch a few minutes of archived footage where the late Peter Jennings of ABC News describes Patti's incredible efforts to save her animals. She proudly watches the video and points out to a co-worker the names of different animals and flashes back to those hectic and chaotic days of the zoo's history.

As the video wraps up, her desk phone rings. Patti answers and says, "Yes, bring him on up." Moments later, through the office door comes a beautiful (yet frightening) Eurasian lynx that appeared quite able to tackle me to the ground and claw my brains out. Instead, it hops up on Patti's desk chair and lets me get close enough to take a photo and even pet him. Go figure.

It was one last treat on an anything-but-normal tour with an anything-but-normal woman. If I walked away with any lessons learned, it was that "normal" is completely overrated. And that yes, humanity is still just fine.

DAD'S COMPUTER

Once a year, I invite my dad to join me on one of my road trips. When I travel, I typically bring along equipment for a variety of productions. For radio or podcasting, I have a digital recorder. Video requires camera equipment like lights, tripods, and wireless microphones. I usually bring along an iPad and at least one laptop computer. Thankfully, as digital technology becomes more advanced, many of these things become more compact and easier to manage. Which is important, since I typically work alone. My most important gear can fit into a backpack, giving me free hands to carry a tripod or a notebook.

When my dad joins me, there's only one piece of equipment he brings along: the world's most pitiful laptop computer. I'm not even sure when he bought it, but it's a constant source of frustration and sometimes comedy. I give credit to anyone not born in the era of computers who makes an effort to learn and use technology when they could easily claim ignorance. For that reason, I try to be helpful when I get the frequent calls about Dad's computer. Early on, it was the expected questions: "What button do I press?" "What's a browser?" "Why won't it turn on?" "It says I'm not connected!"

When I tell this particular story at speaking engagements, I like to ask the audience if this sounds familiar. Sometimes, in a group of mostly seniors, nobody will raise their hand until I lovingly tell them they're all liars. Then, feeling guilty, they laugh and admit they've asked all of these very questions.

Well, one summer, we headed west to tackle a bucket list item —the Beartooth Scenic Byway. The route is about 70 miles long, starting from Red Lodge, Montana, and ending in Cooke City, Montana, at the northeast entrance to Yellowstone National

Park. It takes about two hours to complete, longer if you stop to take pictures or pull off the road to soak in the incredible views.

I often tell people that it's the only place in America where you truly feel like you're standing on another planet. The reaction is always the same: the folks who have never been there sort of chuckle or roll their eyes. But the ones who have taken the drive and have experienced it in person always nod their heads in agreement. It's truly incredible.

For this experience we were staying two nights in Billings. One thing you should know is that, on most occasions when I explore a new destination, the local tourism office will help find me a place to stay while I'm in town. It's one of the perks of being a travel journalist. Though truthfully, I would never be able to do what I do if it weren't the case. Typically, the places I stay can vary wildly. It might be at a brand-new, state-of-the-art property a town is dying to showcase. It may be one of the more well-known hotel chains or it could be a bed and breakfast, which is not uncommon in some smaller communities.

On this particular trip, I received word that there were several large events happening in Billings, resulting in a scarcity of vacant hotel rooms. Reservations were made for a property called the Dude Rancher Lodge. My first clue that trouble was imminent should have been when the lady in charge of tourism told me how nice the new carpet looked in the lobby. Turns out, that was the only thing that looked nice. Red flag #2 was when they handed me the key to the room; it was an actual key!

The motel was similar to what you might have found along Historic Route 66. Once inside the room, we found a mixture of old bricks and wooden paneling, pillows that were thinner than a sheet of copy paper, and towels that belonged in the "before" scene of a Clorox commercial.

It was literally the only place in town to stay for the night, so we sucked it up and made the most of it. Neither of us got much sleep as the sound of guests filling up buckets with ice from the machine echoed through the inner hallway. The next morning, we discovered the guest next door had been using the ice all night long to fill coolers that were piled into the back of a van. God only knows what he was preserving.

As we got set to hit the road for our day exploring the Beartooth Highway, I told my dad that I was bringing all of my stuff with us, even though we'd be returning later that afternoon. I wasn't comfortable leaving behind anything other than dirty clothes and a phone charger. There was just something about this place, a sort of bad news vibe that I was feeling, and I decided to be safe rather than sorry. So I began to bring my belongings to the car—my suitcase, all of my equipment, and even my shoes.

My dad, the eternal optimist, says, "Oh, it'll be fine. I'm going to leave my laptop here."

So off we go. Our day was amazing. I couldn't take enough pictures, or stop the car enough times to soak in the insane amount of beauty found on this magnificent drive. We would park and walk out to explore streams, and we would stand in open fields overlooking hills and colorful landscapes we'd never seen anywhere else in America.

We spent close to eight hours exploring, twice the amount of time we were told to set aside for the experience. At about 5:00 P.M., we headed back to the motel. We pulled into the parking lot and into a space in front of our room when we both noticed something. The door to our room was partially opened.

My first thought was that an employee must have not pulled the door closed enough after cleaning, but we noticed that nothing had been cleaned. Beds were still the same mess we left behind. It was clear that someone had broken into our room.

Now a bit uneasy, we started to look around for anything that could be missing. I glanced at the wooden desk in the room and laughed.

Still sitting there in plain sight was my dad's laptop computer.

I looked over and said to him, "Do you see now what a piece of junk that is? Someone broke in here today looking for valuables, saw your computer, and didn't even bother to touch it."

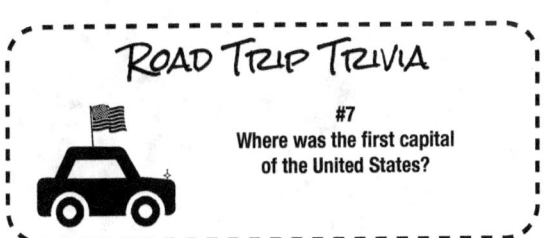

ROAD TRIP TRIVIA

#7
Where was the first capital of the United States?

MORE TO EXPLORE...
The Fred Rogers Center at Saint Vincent College is free and open to the general public.

In Mr. Rogers' hometown of Latrobe, Pennsylvania

WON'T YOU BE MY NEIGHBOR?

Even though I watched *Mister Rogers' Neighborhood* on PBS as a child, I never gave him much thought as an adult. Sure, I remembered him as the guy with all of those sweaters, and I always thought that little trolley he talked to was kind of cool, but that was about it. It wasn't until a road trip through Pennsylvania that I realized what a great angel of a human Mr. Rogers really was.

In 2018, which marked the fiftieth anniversary of his television program, America showed a renewed interest in Fred Rogers. The film *Won't You Be My Neighbor* was called one of the greatest documentaries in decades. It featured behind-the-scenes footage and personal interviews with the people who had known him best.

His long-running children's program was produced in Pittsburgh, at the local PBS affiliate, WQED. The studio wasn't big enough to do an entire episode, so they shot it in segments. They would tape the puppet segments in the castle, tree, clock, and other notable "make-believe" scenes in one day. Then they'd paint the floor and film the scenes in Mr. Rogers's living room and kitchen on another day.

Karen Myers, who handles communications at the Fred Rogers Center, told me about being in the studio shortly after the program wrapped its thirty-first season and final episode. "I remember looking down, wondering how many hundreds of layers of paint must be on the floor," she said. After all, they just kept painting and repainting, over and over, all of those years.

The inevitable question of what to do with over thirty years of props, puppets, and set pieces prompted most of the materials to be donated around town. The Children's Museum of Pittsburgh,

The Heinz History Center, and even the Pittsburgh airport have memorabilia from the sound stage.

Most of the scripts, handwritten notes, photos, and even fan letters wound up in the Fred Rogers Archive at Saint Vincent College. There are more than 16,000 pieces of material related to Rogers' personal and professional life on site. The material includes all of the fan mail that he received over the years. And, according to archivist Emily Urchin, he personally responded to each letter.

Fred McFeely Rogers was born in Latrobe, a small community about an hour southeast of Pittsburgh. His long ties to Saint Vincent College helped secure the location of his archive and the Fred Rogers Center, which was established in 2003. The center has a public exhibit that displays the original main puppets from *Mister Rogers' Neighborhood*—including King Friday, X the Owl, Queen Sarah, Lady Elaine, and Daniel the Tiger. The exhibit also displays some of Fred's sweaters, hand-sewn by his mother, and—of course—the Neighborhood Trolley.

Rogers passed away shortly before the center was off and running. Sadly, he was never able to enjoy a living room space that was designed for him where he could greet and visit with guests. The space, not part of the public exhibit, also houses Fred's personal piano.

The piano was a birthday gift from his grandmother, who sent a young Fred Rogers to pick one from the local music store. Never did she imagine that the one he'd pick was a concert grand Steinway piano, easily the most expensive one on display. She kept true to her word and bought him the piano; it's where he would wind up composing all of the songs used on the TV show.

Everyone always wants to know if Mr. Rogers was the same on-camera as he was off-camera. The short answer is: Yes. The long answer is: Yes, and there'll never be another person quite like him.

While traveling, a detour sign may not be a welcome sight. However, every road has the potential to lead you to interesting places, amusing people, and hidden gems that are off the beaten path. This detour section shares some of my favorite road trip songs, top museums to visit, and the answers to some frequently asked road trip questions.

BILL'S ULTIMATE ROAD TRIP PLAYLIST

"Born Free" by Kid Rock

"Rock Steady" by Aretha Franklin

"Don't Stop Believing" by Journey

"Take Me Home, Country Roads" by John Denver

"Eastbound and Down" by Jerry Reed

"Cold Sweat" by James Brown

"Born to Run" by Bruce Springsteen

"The Power of Love" by Huey Lewis & The News

"Holiday Road" by Lindsey Buckingham

"Mustang Sally" by Wilson Pickett

"Ticket to Ride" by The Beatles

"Love Shack" by The B-52s

"Take a Back Road" by Rodney Atkins

"Six Days on the Road" by Sawyer Brown

"Ramblin' Man" by The Allman Brothers Band

A rock and roll sculpture in Bristol, Virginia.

You can tour a presidential aircraft in Dayton, Ohio, like this former SAM-26000.

TOP 10 FAVORITE MUSEUMS

#1 NATIONAL WWII MUSEUM
New Orleans, Louisiana

A masterfully told story of WWII and how the incredible American military helped save the world from evil. Be sure to watch the 4D film narrated by Tom Hanks, which is one of the most impressive productions I've ever seen.

#2 CHILDREN'S MUSEUM OF INDIANAPOLIS
Indianapolis, Indiana

Hands down, this is the greatest children's museum in the U.S. Thoughtfully designed with engaging exhibits for all ages.

#3 STRONG NATIONAL MUSEUM OF PLAY
Rochester, New York

If you want to re-connect with your childhood, the Strong Museum of Play is home to the National Toy Hall of Fame and features an entire floor full of video games. Every guest will see things relating to their childhood.

#4 NATIONAL MUSEUM OF TOYS & MINIATURES
Kansas City, Missouri

I was dragging my feet the first time someone took me here. I now try to make a visit every chance I can. The miniature displays are incredible.

TOP 10 FAVORITE MUSEUMS

#5   CITY MUSEUM
St. Louis, Missouri

There is no describing the City Museum other than to say there's a school bus and Ferris wheel on top of the roof along with a giant slide. When I tell people I am from St. Louis, this is the place people most often want to talk about.

#6   CENTER FOR PUPPETRY ARTS
Atlanta, Georgia

If you're a fan of puppets—especially Jim Henson's The Muppets, you will love this place! It has some of the most well-known puppets on display including Kermit The Frog, Gumby, and other instantly recognizable characters from television and film.

#7   AMERICAN SIGN MUSEUM
Cincinnati, Ohio

This hidden gem tells the story of America through signs. If you love neon signs, you'll be blown away at all the amazing displays.

#8   HENRY FORD MUSEUM
Dearborn, Michigan

Where else on Earth can you see the Wright Brothers' bicycle shop, the bus Rosa Parks made famous, and the chair President Lincoln was assassinated in? You'll need comfortable shoes and two or three days to see everything here.

TOP 10 FAVORITE MUSEUMS

#9 NATIONAL MUSEUM OF THE U.S. AIR FORCE
Dayton, Ohio

This is one of the best free museums in America. Four massive airplane hangars house all of the great military planes, in the order of their time in service. Getting to tour a former presidential aircraft used by George H. W. Bush and Bill Clinton is a highlight.

#10 CRYSTAL BRIDGES MUSEUM OF ART
Bentonville, Arkansas

If you don't consider yourself an "art lover," this may be the place that changes your mind. Inside this stunning building, exhibits are displayed in fun, enlightening ways that will make you appreciate art like never before. Make time to walk on the outdoor trails. Admission is free.

ROAD TRIP Q&A

Favorite snack?
I always keep granola bars and a Ziploc bag of Cheez-It crackers in my car.

Best time to drive?
I hate waking up early, but the best time to start a road trip is before the sun comes up! Beat the local traffic and use the extra time to make a few unplanned stops along the way.

Souvenirs?
I don't really collect anything these days. However, a great idea if you frequently take road trips is to look for Christmas ornaments. They don't have to be expensive. You can always find something small that can hang on your tree at the end of the year!

Pet peeve?
Definitely people who text while driving. They are always swerving into another lane, or driving too slow. I think it's incredibly dangerous and selfish. Sadly, there are so many of these people on the road who think they're talented enough to both text and drive. Newsflash: you're not. (Runner up: people who don't use their blinker!)

What's on the radio?
I've always had a rule in my car: the driver picks the songs. I prefer music in the daytime but enjoy listening to talk programs in the evening to keep me engaged and alert.

ROAD TRIP Q&A

Something you frequently need but don't always have?
Coins! I'm spoiled to live in a town where parking is typically free. It doesn't hurt to throw a roll of quarters in your glove compartment for when you need them.

Most embarrassing moment in a car?
In 2004, I had a job as a chaperone for the Playboy Playmate of the Year. I would go to various cities and travel with her to events. Once at the Denver International Airport, we were parking and I couldn't find the button to roll the window down to take a ticket for the parking garage. (We were in a rental car.) I tried to open the door but I had parked too close so I couldn't get my arm out far enough. By the time I finally figured out where the button was (on the steering wheel of all places) people had lined up behind us and were honking their horns. Not my proudest moment, as the Playmate of the Year sat a few inches away, watching me sweat.

Neat or messy?
Neat. Some might use the word "spotless." One time I interviewed a tour guide in Gettysburg who took visitors around the battlefield. It was a windy day, so we recorded our interview inside my car, just a few yards from where Lincoln delivered the Gettysburg Address. As we wrapped up the conversation, I asked the man if he had anything else he wanted to share with the audience. To my surprise, the man said, "Your listeners should know—Bill has the cleanest car I have ever been in."

ROAD TRIP Q&A

In case of an emergency?
I'm definitely not as prepared as I should be but I do keep a handful of things in my vehicle—just in case: a warm blanket, pillow, bright flashlight, a knife, a bag of napkins, water, sunscreen, umbrella, ice scraper, and an ABBA CD. I'll be honest, I don't know why that's in there.

Any tips on making road trip plans?
Once you've determined where you want to go, consider using the local CVB (Convention and Visitor Bureau) in each city or town for tips and advice about where to stay, eat, etc. A CVB is a free resource staffed by locals who know the area best and can provide valuable information you may not find in other places. They can often tell you the best times to visit, what and where to avoid, and if there are construction sites or big events happening that might interfere with your plans.

ROAD TRIP FUN FACTS

1.
Kansas is NOT the flattest state in the U.S. Florida, Illinois, North Dakota, Louisiana, and Minnesota are all flatter.

2.
The largest privately owned home in America is the Biltmore Estate in Asheville, North Carolina. There are 250 rooms, which includes 35 bedrooms, 43 bathrooms, and 65 fireplaces.

3.
Despite Illinois being known as the "Land of Lincoln"—Honest Abe was actually born in Kentucky.

4.
Lake Michigan is the only "Great Lake" located entirely within the United States.

5.
Le Mars, Iowa, is known as the "Ice Cream Capital of the World" for its ties to Blue Bunny Ice Cream.

6.
The Statue of Liberty is actually located in New Jersey.

7.
It's a myth that the U.S. Interstate system was designed to land planes in the event of a war.

ROAD TRIP FUN FACTS

8.
Alaska's coastline is longer than that of all of the other 49 states combined.

9.
The federal government owns 85 percent of Nevada.

10.
Yellowstone is the oldest national park in the U.S.

11.
The Smithsonian National Air and Space Museum is the most-visited museum in the U.S.

12.
The last time the Liberty Bell rang was in 1846, for George Washington's birthday.

13.
The current U.S. flag was designed by a 17-year-old for a school project. His teacher gave him a "B," and called it a mediocre.

14.
Crater Lake, at 1,932 feet deep, is the deepest lake in America.

15.
There are 182 places in the U.S. with "Christmas" in their names.

MORE TO EXPLORE...
Another popular tourist stop in Oxford is Rowan Oak, the mansion of American author William Faulkner.

On the football field at Ole Miss in Oxford, Mississippi.

SOUTH DAKOTA

The great thing about travel is that the road doesn't always lead where you think it will. After all, as the old saying goes: "Man plans, God laughs."

Sometimes, the moments that stand out most are the ones you assumed would be an afterthought. I never in a million years could have imagined that a tiny town in South Dakota would be the most consequential place I'd visit on my journey across America.

Honestly, this is not a story that I planned to share. In fact, even though it's in the middle of this book, it's the very last addition, after some reflection and internal debate. Truth is that even the stories that make us uncomfortable, still remain part of our history. For better or worse, every experience is part of life.

While working on travel plans for the summer of 2016, I made the decision to visit Mount Rushmore. Initially, I had planned to stop in Rapid City, which is about an hour away from the famous landmark. Those plans fell through a couple of weeks before the road trip and I found myself scrambling for an alternative stop.

The state of South Dakota has a great tourism department and they offered several suggestions. At the time, I wasn't familiar with any of the places they listed. So I sent e-mails to all three of them. Only one place bothered to respond: a small town called Custer.

When I rolled into town (the last stop on a two-week road trip), I was invited to take a helicopter ride to see the region's famed Black Hills. We lifted off despite strong winds, taking a beautiful but bumpy route over the terrain and a special detour to catch my very first glimpse of Mount Rushmore.

Little did I know that one of the other passengers taking in the views from high above would be the woman with whom I would plan to spend the rest of my life.

Later that evening, we played a round of miniature golf, the first of many games she'd win over time. I didn't care that much about the golf, or the fact that everything in town seemed to shut down by 6:00 P.M. Instead, I was completely smitten and spent the rest of the night pretending that we both didn't know I was headed home the next morning.

As someone who interviews quite a few people, I'd learned to listen carefully and pay attention to small details. She had noted in our long conversation that she loved donuts. On my way out of town, I made one last stop and surprised her with treats from the local bakery. She hugged me and begged me not to go. This may seem a bit silly, or even something you'd expect from a kid in junior high. But walking out the door and driving away from this girl I had just met was one of the toughest things I've ever had to do.

We kept in touch, talking on the phone, texting, and using FaceTime. She was now fourteen hours away from my hometown. Just eight days after I had left her, she purchased a plane ticket to visit me in St. Louis.

We explored the town and I took her to as many of the sites as possible. A ride to the top of the Gateway Arch, a Blues hockey game, and a ride on the Ferris wheel atop the City Museum. We shared our adventures on social media and soon became the love story that everyone wanted to follow.

I'd visit her for weeks at a time where we often did amusing live videos. On the night before Thanksgiving, we did our own cooking show of sorts, illustrating how to make a turkey out of crackers, cheese, and pepperoni. She was shy and I was the goofball. Eventually, she came out of her shell and relished the online broadcasts.

She also played tour guide when possible. One morning, we explored Custer State Park where we found ourselves trapped inside her car by a herd of hungry bison. With no cell service and no place to turn, we nervously watched as these massive animals licked salt off the exterior of the vehicle.

I learned the lifestyle of South Dakotans, from driving in blizzards to quirky attractions like Wall Drug or the Corn Palace. I met lots of friendly people in town and learned to appreciate some aspects of small-town living that I'd never known before.

When we weren't physically together, we talked every day, sometimes for hours. We had our inside jokes. We laughed, we debated, and we made plans for the future. She didn't know it, but nine months after we met, I had bought an engagement ring. This was the person I had always hoped to meet. I made arrangements and crafted a scheme to propose. It was clever and heartfelt.

About two weeks before I planned to propose, I was on a trip exploring towns along the Missouri River. Excited and a bit nervous, I shared my plans with fellow travel writers. They were supportive and calming. Marriage is a big deal to everyone, but it's a particularly big deal when you've pretty much assumed you'd never find the perfect match.

May 1, 2017: the trip was over and I was winding down in my hotel room in Kansas City, Kansas. The next day, I'd travel by train back to St. Louis. A storm was brewing, in more ways than one. Loud thunder, heavy rain, and incredible lightning filled the night sky.

I made my regular evening call to South Dakota, no different than any other night. Except that it did turn out to be different. Without warning, after a brief conversation, she broke up with me.

As though right on cue—within seconds of the call ending—the power in the entire hotel went out. So there I sat, all alone in the dark, far from home. I only remember the date because it turned out to be the worst night of my life. Grown men aren't supposed to cry, and if you do cry, you're certainly not supposed to admit it. But I did. I cried and cried and cried.

When the power came back on late in the evening, I shared online that my relationship had ended. I don't recall my exact words but I wished her the best and asked for positive thoughts or even a prayer. Anything that might help the hurt I felt inside.

The next morning, I checked my phone while sitting in a waiting room at Kansas City's Union Station. More than 300 text messages were waiting for me from family and friends. Word had spread to my radio listeners and readers across the country. They too sent e-mails. My voicemail box was full. It was overwhelming.

Tears streamed down my face again as I sat alone in this bustling train depot, reading the most kind, touching, thoughtful messages I'd ever read. Who knows? Maybe this was the plan all along: to be reminded that I'm cared for and loved.

When I returned home, the first thing that I did was write myself a letter. I described how I felt and noted that one day, I'd open it, read it, and realize that a broken heart would eventually mend. It took over a year for me to find the strength to open that envelope and read those words. Even now, some days I think I read it too soon.

The reality is that some stories don't get the ending you choose. After all, God laughs at our plans.

At Cracker Barrel in Lebanon, Tennessee, with one of the company's first ten investors—Jack Cato.

THE CRACKER BARREL GOLD CARD

At the Cracker Barrel restaurant in Lebanon, Tennessee, a new friend kindly picks up the check after dinner. Jack Cato flashes a rarely seen, gold credit card toward the cashier—and just like that, the bill disappears. Mr. Cato gets free Cracker Barrel meals for life. It's one of the perks when you're one of the company's first investors.

Cracker Barrel, now a national brand with more than 600 locations, is known for its "Old Country Store" and home-style food. At age eighty-six, Mr. Cato remains sharp and full of stories, including tales from the early days of the business. He coughed up $10,000 for 20,000 shares of Cracker Barrel, along with nine other individuals from Wilson County. (twenty thousand shares would cost more than $3 million today.)

The two of us spend part of the afternoon visiting at a small circular table in a modest, outdated building where he once worked on televisions. Mr. Cato talks about being approached by Danny Evins, who was looking for ten local investors to expand the single Cracker Barrel store. He admits that he thought it was a crazy idea, and that there really was no business plan in place.

As I sat there listening to his stories, he'd get up and grab a random item from a nearby table. "I invested in this thing," he'd say. The items ranged from high-tech gas cans to household gadgets. Apparently, he's got a knack for picking winners.

He was also thrifty, a trait commonly found in people who have made a very good living. Before we leave for dinner, he yells to his wife across the room, "Do you know we have sandwiches in the fridge?" His quiet, unassuming wife nods as Jack tells me about this deal he found at a fast food chain. "Three sandwiches for five dollars: can you believe that?" All I could think of was that this guy can probably afford to buy the entire franchise and yet here he is, tickled to death over cheap chicken.

Lebanon is still the headquarters for Cracker Barrel and its presence is well known. Mr. Cato, a familiar face to everyone on their beautiful campus, walks me through the warehouse where all of those antiques are stored. Each item hanging from the walls of your favorite Cracker Barrel store—a painting, bottle, tin sign, or instrument—everything comes from this warehouse. They scour the country looking for pieces to decorate new locations. On the day of our visit, they were shipping pallets of antiques to Las Vegas for new stores.

Before dropping me off at my car, Mr. Cato reels off an endless amount of fun facts, some in the form of trivia questions. "Do you know how many biscuits Cracker Barrel makes each year?" he asks. "Two-hundred million!" He shares that the company sells more than 200,000 of their iconic rocking chairs, and uses 53 million bottles of syrup.

The one question he couldn't answer was how to solve that peg game on the table.

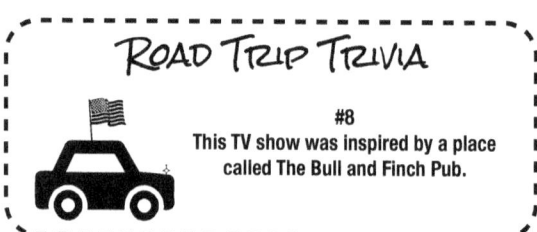

ROAD TRIP TRIVIA

#8
This TV show was inspired by a place called The Bull and Finch Pub.

HOME SWEET HOME

Even before I started traveling professionally, I learned that people are generally fascinated by seeing the homes of complete strangers. What's the first thing you think of when a neighbor's house is up for sale? I mean, besides, "Oh crap, I hope some weirdos don't move in down the street." If we're being honest, most people immediately want to take a glance inside.

Homes that were once occupied by someone famous featured in a film, or homes that carry some sort of historical significance are always hot spots for tourists. I've toured many of these places. Some are fascinating, while others are total duds.

I've personally always enjoyed seeing the former homes of American presidents. Both Eisenhower's childhood home in Kansas and his final residence in Gettysburg are favorites of mine. Walking through the tiny white house in Abilene, you get a sense of how he was molded into a future military icon. While in Gettysburg, you get a sense of what a normal, regular person he was at heart.

Eisenhower would enjoy his meals at home on a TV tray in his favorite recliner, near the back sunroom. He had a remote control to manage flipping among the three or four channels he had to choose from. A tour guide pointed out that he preferred people calling him "General" instead of "President" after he left Washington and returned to Pennsylvania.

It's in these homes that we get a better look at who was really in charge of the family. Mamie Eisenhower, who lived in the home until her death in 1979, loved all things pink. Imagine being one of the most revered generals in U.S. history, sleeping at night in a bedroom that was completely pink from the bed sheets and pillows to the curtains and the flowers along the

MORE TO EXPLORE...
President Eisenhower's childhood home is located on the same campus as the library and museum.

window. Outside of their bedroom, there was no escape. The bathroom was full of pink, including a closet loaded with pink towels and wash cloths.

The home is fairly modest, aside from some displays of gifts from world leaders in the living room. One great perk was a putting green on the back lawn that was installed for the PGA.

At one time, the public probably viewed the home as a "mansion." By today's standards it isn't. It's not that different from Elvis Presley's Memphis estate, Graceland. Graceland, which was named long before Elvis purchased the property in 1957, cost the singer $102,500. The mansion is 10,266 square feet. In terms of size, it's certainly comparable to many homes of today's top celebrities. However, once you step inside…not so much.

One thing every guest notes is the green shag carpet in several rooms of the house. The kitchen is not impressive at all and the bedrooms (at least the ones you're allowed to view) are not big. The basement of the Graceland mansion is kind of cool though; who wouldn't love their own game room or living room with three televisions?

Elvis is not the only musician to have his home turned into a tourist attraction, though it's certainly the most popular. (Graceland is second only to the White House in terms of visitors.) Former country music star Conway Twitty welcomed guests into his mansion known as "Twitty City" just outside of Nashville. Former star Barbara Mandrell, who was among the most popular musical acts of the 1980s, also opened the doors to her former home. Loretta Lynn still welcomes guests to the ranch she lived in for twenty-two years in the town of Hurricane Mills, Tennessee.

In the small Missouri town of Marceline, tourists drive by and admire the childhood home of Walt Disney. It's in this community where Disney began to create lovable characters and dream of big things, things larger than anything possible in a town that still has only about 2,000 residents. Disney's former home is privately owned and not open for tours, but that doesn't stop gawkers from posing for photos on the front lawn.

While seeing a former home is exciting to some, it's even more exciting for tourists to drive by the current residence of someone famous. In southern California, it's big business for sightseeing companies to take visitors around places where they can gawk at the homes of movie stars and notable personalities. Having lived in southern California before, I remember buying one of those maps and trying to locate some of the mansions with friends. Many of the streets are public and driving down them isn't against the law, but you still have the feeling you're doing something wrong. So it becomes a quick glance here or there.

Only once have I gone into a notable house and felt so uncomfortable that I left almost as soon as I walked in the front door. House on the Rock in Spring Green, Wisconsin, is a popular destination because of its peculiar design and collections. Alex Jordon, Jr. built the home, which includes dozens of rooms, many only lit by the light of windows and bizarre displays like automated musical instruments. The supposed largest indoor carousel, complete with 269 different animals (not a single horse), is near the end of the public tour. I never made it remotely close to that point, as I felt like I had entered into some sort of a nightmare or satanic church. I found the place incredibly disturbing and couldn't get out of there fast enough.

Remarkably, it's one of the most visited attractions in the entire state of Wisconsin.

After Aretha Franklin passed away in 2018, fresh attention was

MORE TO EXPLORE...

On a haunted house tour with author David Domine, in Old Louisville, KY...known as "America's Most Haunted Neighborhood."

given to her childhood home in Memphis. The unassuming, partially boarded up house still draws visitors. The Indiana childhood home of Michael Jackson and the Jackson family draws tourists, despite being in a particularly sketchy neighborhood. A sign sits out in front of the house, but no tours are given. Homes like these seem to be interesting to people because it reminds them that in our country, many people work their way to fame or fortune without being born with it.

The Winchester Mystery House in San Jose is one of the most bizarre, and potentially haunted, houses I've toured. I featured it in my book *100 Things to Do in America Before You Die*, simply because it's just so strange. Built in 1884 by Sarah Winchester, construction on the property continued twenty-four hours a day, seven days a week, never stopping until her death in 1922. Rumors persisted that the spirits of people killed by Winchester guns could be found in the home. In an effort to ward off the spirits, the mansion has staircases that lead to nowhere, windows overlooking other rooms, and other architectural oddities that certainly make it a unique.

Old Louisville, Kentucky, is often called "America's Most Haunted Neighborhood." This was one of my first trips when I became a travel writer. They claim to have more Victorian-style homes than any other place in the U.S. They are all over the place, and they are really stunning. They also claim to have lots of ghost activity and swear that many of the homes have had (and still have) ghosts that pop up on occasion.

THE DAY I SPENT IN PRISON

Ray Miller is eighty-two years old. He's been a tour guide at the now-vacant Missouri State Penitentiary for the past ten years. At his age, he has plenty of stories he could share with visitors. However, these days, all he wants to talk about is prison.

"Oh yeah, I've seen a ghost here," Ray tells a curious visitor. "He had a white lab coat, white pants, and was holding a clipboard."

The ghost story was just part of more than thirty minutes' worth of tales about the prison's history and the many characters that wound up inside these concrete walls and metal bars. Of course, that's a long time to sit still in a dark, dreary, freezing-cold (most of the guests were wearing coats and gloves) slammer. However, nobody seemed to mind, as Mr. Miller's prison tales became more and more intriguing.

Missouri State Penitentiary held some of the most dangerous prisoners in the country and also some of the most infamous. James Earl Ray, once an inmate here, escaped in a bread truck. He'd later go on to assassinate Dr. Martin Luther King, Jr.

One inmate went on to achieve great fame in the sports world. Charles "Sonny" Liston was released in 1952 and worked his way to world heavyweight champion. (A cardboard cut-out of Liston stands outside of his former cell.)

After achieving fame, he returned to the prison where he first learned the art of boxing and challenged the inmates to a match. Mr. Miller notes, "He promised to take on six guys but he warned them ahead of time that they were all going to get knocked out. And he was right. He clobbered all six of them."

Not all of the stories from within the walls of Missouri State Penitentiary had happy endings. In fact, most didn't.

On "death row" at the Missouri State Penitentiary in Jefferson City, Missouri.

The conditions for prisoners were atrocious, even for those of the bunch who had committed the worst offenses. At its most crowded point, as many as eight prisoners were jammed into a single cell, which had just enough space to fit two small cots, a sink, and a toilet.

In the early days of the prison, medical care for inmates barely existed. One example shared on the tour was about a man who had completely swollen tonsils and couldn't breathe. With no one to provide emergency surgery, another inmate offered to cut the man's tonsils out with a razor blade. He did. The man bled to death outside of his cell.

Down below the prison is a dungeon where the worst offenders or trouble makers would wind up. We walked down a set of slick concrete stairs and through a narrow door that led to several solitary confinement chambers. As a group we stood inside, lights out, and experienced what a prisoner would feel. One inmate was known to take a button off of his shirt and throw it around the cold, pitch-dark room where he would then search and try to locate it. He claimed doing this activity over and over kept him from going insane.

Often, the inmates in the dungeon had two buckets of water to share. One for fresh water and one for waste. Being in the dark, sometimes you didn't always know which was which. And God forbid if someone would knock over one of the buckets.

The general tour includes a walk into death row and then eventually to the gas chamber. On the sidewalk leading into the gas chamber you step over a large cross on the ground. Both experiences are chilling.

One lighter moment from the mix of stories came when we learned about a former prison program that was designed to help troubled youth in the area. The idea was to have inmates who posed no real danger interact with kids in an effort to scare them straight—and keep them from also becoming prisoners one day.

During one of the programs, a former mobster was speaking to a group of these juveniles when one young man cockily burst out, "So what are you in here for?" The mobster turned and brought the kid closer, leaned down to eye level, and said, without hesitation, "I drowned a kid about your size in a bathtub."

Of course, he never actually drowned any children but the tall tale certainly assured this particular kid (and probably those standing nearby) that he was never going to do anything that put him behind the walls of that prison. In a twisted way, the program was a success.

Mr. Miller ended his tour chatting with guests who had additional questions. He gleefully talked about a recent visit to a typically off-limits section of the property. He told another man about other prisons he's been to and which ones he'd still like to see.

All I kept thinking was: One prison is enough.

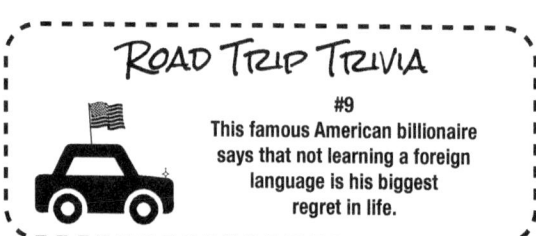

ROAD TRIP TRIVIA

#9
This famous American billionaire says that not learning a foreign language is his biggest regret in life.

EXPENSIVE JUNK

Jerry Bradley sits a foot away from me, in an old waiting room chair from the RCA Records building on Music Row in Nashville. It's one of hundreds of objects he refers to as "junk" in his Mount Juliet man-cave. At one time, this was the site of the historic Bradley Barn, a recording studio and facility for Nashville's biggest stars. Bradley is the former vice president of the record label; he is responsible for dozens of hit records and the success of many well-known country music artists.

Like a grandfather whose stories captivate even a kid with the attention span of a house fly, Mr. Bradley serves up tale after tale that leaves you wanting more and more.

He tells the story of signing a little-known group called Alabama. At the time, they were on a tiny label and nobody in Nashville wanted them. Bradley, wanting a group as part of his label's catalog of artists, signed them anyway. The group became one of the biggest selling bands in music history, with over seventy-five million albums sold and more than forty number one hit songs.

Each piece of Mr. Bradley's junk has an incredible story behind it. An autographed black-and-white photo of what appears to be astronauts on the moon is sitting on the floor, propped up against the wall. Mr. Bradley tells me how he produced a cassette for the guys who went to the moon so they'd have something to listen to on their trip.

A wall of gold records indicates how many songs and artists have been influenced by Jerry Bradley and his father, Owen Bradley, also a famous music producer. As I challenge his definition of the many rare items in his collection, he finally concedes, "Okay, it's expensive junk."

The first one to catch my eye is a gold record for *Wanted! The Outlaws*—an album known to insiders as a monumental production that in many ways changed the music business. Mr. Bradley shares stories (and headaches) of getting together the artists—Willie Nelson, Waylon Jennings, Jessi Colter, and Tompall Glasser—to get the album produced.

"A lawyer got involved; Tompall wouldn't sign the papers to release the album and so I called him. I said, 'This is Jerry Bradley and I have two album covers—one that has your picture on it and one that doesn't. You have ten minutes to bring me the signed contract.'"

Of course, Mr. Glasser came running into Bradley's office with the signed contract.

The property where the Bradley Barn was once located is absolutely beautiful and peaceful, surrounded by nothing but trees and fresh air. It's no wonder so many artists wanted to escape the bright lights of Nashville and come here to record their songs. Conway Twitty, Loretta Lynn, Kitty Wells, Dolly Parton, Dinah Shore, Burl Ives, and so many others came here to sing and cement their place in music history.

Mr. Bradley talks about his dad, who taught him everything he needed to know to be a success in the entertainment business. "If he told me to sweep the floor, I'd sweep the floor. But before long he had me turning knobs."

A wire in a fluorescent light started a fire that would burn Bradley Barn down in 1982, on his dad's sixty-fifth birthday. Its replacement, though much smaller, was still used as a recording studio for many years. Today, it's mostly storage with a small living room set-up. In one cluttered room, a dusty leather sofa rests in the corner with boxes on top. Mr. Bradley tells a tale about Dolly Parton sitting there in the 1980s.

As we wrap up our interview, Jerry points at my recorder and

MORE TO EXPLORE...
In Nashville, be sure to tour the historic Ryman Auditorium.

With former RCA Records vice president Jerry Bradley.

says "You'll want to get this one on tape," and proceeds to tell me another great story. He talks about the day Waylon Jennings brought him three songs and he hated all of them.

"You don't look interested," exclaimed Jennings.

He concurred that he wasn't thrilled even though they'd probably still sell a couple hundred thousand copies. At that point, Jennings stood up and sang what would become one of the most well-known country music songs of all time.

Standing up from behind his desk Bradley yelled, "Whatever you do, go record that tonight and throw one of those other three in the trash."

That was the birth of a tune called "Mamas Don't Let Your Babies Grow Up To Be Cowboys."

ROAD QURIK

Jim Bolin is a soft-spoken guy who loves his tiny town of Casey, Illinois. Located along I-70—almost exactly halfway between Indianapolis and St. Louis—Casey is like so many other small towns, in Illinois and all across America. A single stoplight, one or two gas stations, and a population of about 3,000 people.

Mr. Bolin's family business, Bolin Enterprises, is based here. The company, which employs 250 workers, does large-scale maintenance projects on pipelines. Using recycled materials from work sites, Jim and his co-workers have produced at least eight different "world record" roadside attractions in their town.

The first attraction was the world's tallest wind chime. Completed in 2011, Bolin's first crack at building a larger-than-life object stemmed from a desire to save his small town. He talked to me about drivers flying by, never taking the time to stop and experience the community he grew up in and loves. The wind chime, which stands 56 feet tall, was an idea to get curious drivers to stop and take a look at the town.

It seemed to work. Bolin decided to try something else. Working with the local golf course, he built the world's largest golf tee. It's a whopping 35.5 feet tall and weighs 6,659 pounds. It was unveiled in 2013, which was about the time I first heard of Casey, Illinois. I noticed the sign and decided to pull off of I-70 and check it out. I remember asking a woman at the golf course if she knew how many people stopped in each day just to get a look at the giant tee. She said, "Today, you're number 147."

Sensing that they'd stumbled onto something, Casey set out to be known for not just a couple of big things, but an entire town full of them. There's the world's largest pitchfork, rocking chair, wooden shoes, and—my personal favorite—the world's

Using the world's largest knitting needles in Casey, Illinois.

largest mailbox. The mailbox is 5,743 cubic feet and you can take stairs to climb inside. If you decide to mail a letter while you're up there, a giant red flag goes up along the side and it becomes a real, functioning mailbox.

Some of the items are actually inside local stores. The world's largest knitting needles are placed inside a store called "The Yarn Studio." Jeanette, who owns and runs the store, greeted me when I stopped in Casey on a book tour in 2017. She asked if I wanted to try knitting something with the giant needles. Not being one to turn down a new experience, I walked over to the shop and started knitting! She noted that I was the first person (aside from her) to actually use the 13.75-foot-long needles. Each one weighs 25 pounds and they're completely functional.

Walking along Casey's main street is like stepping into a scene from the film *Honey, I Shrunk The Kids*. And if a local happens to spot you walking the sidewalk or taking photos, they'll probably pull over and hand you a cheat sheet with the exact locations of all the town's attractions. Everyone is quite proud.

These fun, quirky sights are an important part of keeping small towns relevant but also a way to make road trips more enjoyable. Perhaps it started in the days of Route 66 when driving from Chicago to L.A. took a lot of time and certainly had to cause boredom for long stretches of travel.

Most of those sights were the motels and diners. But over the years, roadside attractions like the Blue Whale of Catoosa, near Tulsa, Oklahoma, became popular stops for motorists to stretch their legs, take a break, and take the opportunity to capture a fun photo.

Today, using GPS and specialized phone apps like Roadside America, it's easy to find these quirky or peculiar objects along most any route in the country. Metropolis, Illinois, has the world's tallest Superman statue and Blue Earth, Minnesota, has the world's tallest Jolly Green Giant. Of course, it's not just statues; there's the world's largest baseball bat, dresser drawers, milk bottle, and even the world's tallest easel, which displays a giant Van Gogh replica painting. Oh, and don't forget the world's largest goose, located in Sumner, Missouri.

As for the town of Casey, there are more "big things" on the way. You can walk by the official "big things" workshop, located just behind the wind chime. You'll hear hammers, saws, and drills but never know exactly what big thing is coming next. Guess you'll have to pull off the highway and find out for yourself.

POPEYE'S HOMETOWN

Debbie Brooks has been a Popeye fan for decades. Along with her husband, Mike, they've collected thousands of Popeye trinkets, statues, figures, dolls, and everything else you can imagine. "We have thousands of things that we don't even have room for in the museum," says Brooks as I stroll around their Chester, Illinois, store called Spinach Can Collectibles.

Chester is best known as the hometown of Popeye creator Elzie Segar. Mr. Segar once worked in the same building that Debbie Brooks now uses for her museum, store, and headquarters for the Popeye Fan Club. Segar was a projectionist and even played drums when the building was a movie theater.

Most of the Popeye characters are based on real people including Wimpy, Bluto, and Olive. "People are usually surprised when they find out Olive was actually created a while before Popeye came along," notes Brooks.

Popeye was based on Chester resident Frank Fiegel, who was said to strongly resemble the spinach-eating cartoon character who first debuted in 1929. Mr. Segar introduced a love of spinach into the character's persona after eating it routinely as a child. Segar suffered from leukemia and his parents were convinced that spinach would be a cure. He eventually died from the disease in 1938.

Debbie and Mike Brooks moved to Chester in 1994 and began a quest to help put Chester on the map through its ties to Popeye. Eventually they opened a museum and convinced the town to embrace the cartoon character's legacy and heritage.

Today, the town has thirteen Popeye statues with several more in the works. Billboards and signs with the comic's likeness appear all over town. Even the local police and fire departments use his face on their logos.

Debbie is fearful that Popeye may one day be forgotten, as younger generations aren't being introduced to him the way other cartoon icons have been sewn into pop culture. "They apparently tried to make a new film recently but they took away his pipe and spinach and tried to make him politically correct. It didn't work."

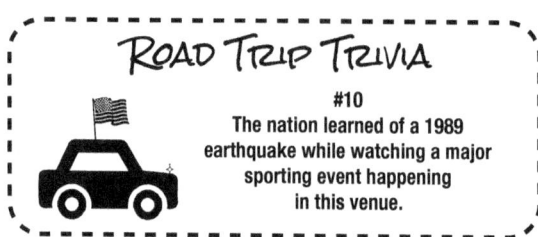

ROAD TRIP TRIVIA

#10
The nation learned of a 1989 earthquake while watching a major sporting event happening in this venue.

SHE DOESN'T WORK HERE ANYMORE

I've always tried to be open and honest with people who follow my travels by sharing all of the good things—as well as the bad—that happen while out on the road. Thankfully, it's pretty rare that I have bad news to report. And, while most of the time, things go as planned, sometimes you run into the occasional roadblock.

Take, for instance, the time I visited the George Jones Museum in Nashville. On that road trip through Tennessee, I was recording an hour-long radio program that consisted of four different segments, highlighting various places of interest. I had finished three segments, and this would be the last one before heading home.

George Jones is considered by many to be the most influential performer in the history of country music. His voice was unlike any other, and ironically, his life and career consisted of all the very elements that make the perfect country music song. His hit songs include "White Lightning," "Finally Friday," "The Grand Tour," and what's often called the saddest country song ever recorded: "He Stopped Loving Her Today."

One thing you should know about me is that I'm very organized and I'm always on time. From a very early age, I learned that it's always important to never be late. This has caused many anxious moments in the car where unforeseen circumstances like traffic, lack of parking, or bad directions have caused me to cut it close. I'm also adamant that I make plans and arrange things ahead of time. Hopping in the car and driving around with no schedule sounds great in theory. In reality, it's a disaster if your job is a writer or broadcaster.

The George Jones Museum had only been open to the public

for a few days when I was scheduled to stop in. Brand new, and unveiled with much fanfare in a bustling part of downtown Nashville, the early reviews indicated it was worth seeing. As I walked in the front door, I introduced myself to a man at the front desk and told him I was there to do an interview. Not surprisingly, he had no idea who I was or that I was scheduled to be there. I told the man that I had set up the visit with the museum's publicist and I went on to name her. He responded, "She doesn't work here anymore." I quickly countered with, "That's interesting. She worked here yesterday."

I moved on to the enormous gift shop where I waited for someone to figure out who I was supposed to interview. After waiting for what seemed like a lifetime, I decided to take matters into my own hands. A door opened and two individuals, a male and a female, walked into the room as they continued their conversation. After you've done this for a while, you start to recognize what kind of people look like they're in charge. I'm right more times than I'm wrong, and so I approached them.

"Excuse me, I'm sorry to bother you, but I am supposed to do a radio segment about the museum here this afternoon," I politely said. The woman bluntly responded, "I don't know anything about this; who did you talk to?" I mentioned the name of the PR gal. "She doesn't work here anymore," the woman quipped. I wanted to respond, "Yeah, that's certainly the word on the street."

Completely disinterested in what I had come to do, the woman said, "Well, you'll just have to come back another time." And this, sports fans, is the moment I lost my cool. As I mentioned before, I am very organized and work very hard to make sure all of my plans are set up ahead of time. This time was no exception, and I had gone through the proper channels and followed the instructions given to me. There are very few things that get me riled up, but I absolutely hate when people waste my time or take advantage of me.

While I never raised my voice, I started to make it known that I was not very happy that I had been asked to wait around, and even less happy that I was being treated so rudely. I told them I was there doing them a favor to promote their new museum and I shouldn't be jumping through hoops to do it. It was probably only a few minutes, but it seemed like an hour of arguing back and forth between these two individuals and me.

Clearly searching for a way out, the man asked, "So what is it exactly that you need?" I took a breath and said, "All I need is for someone to tell me a little bit about what's in the museum, and about the life of George Jones."

Looking over at the woman he said, "Well, she should be able to do that." And it was in this moment that I could feel my head tilt the way a dog does when you ask it a serious question. Something was popping into my head and my brain was starting to make some calculations. I finally realized that I had been standing there, in front of a crowd, arguing with the wife of George Jones.

To her credit, she agreed to sit down with me and do a short interview. I turned on the recorder and began to ask questions. The entire time I sat there, all I could think of was that this woman absolutely hated me. I'm sure she was thinking something similar about me. As our interview started to wind down, her mood started to sweeten and she did what only women in the South can do: she put her hand on my leg and smiled. Absent were the words "Bless your heart," but I knew she didn't hate me anymore.

We wrapped up, I stopped the recorder, and she said, "I'm really sorry I bit your head off earlier." I responded with "Well, I'm sorry I had no idea who you were."

MORE TO EXPLORE...
Check out the painted pianos scattered about the streets of Fort Collins, available for anyone to play!

On the campus of Colorado State University in Fort Collins, Colorado.

OLD, DIRTY, BUMPY ROADS

My family has always had property in what you'd call "the country." You know, a place where the nearest grocery store is thirty miles away, the stars are unlimited in the night sky, and—of course—good luck getting high speed internet. So when they told me that the boyhood home of music legend Johnny Cash was "on a dirt road," I knew what to expect. And I was completely wrong.

The exit sign read "Dyess" as I pulled off of southbound Highway 55, in northeastern Arkansas. About thirty minutes outside of Memphis, the roads here are a combination of dirt, big rocks, and lots of dust. I have never seen dirt roads quite like this. A large brown cloud formed as I drove no more than ten miles an hour, in search of the home where Johnny Cash lived as a kid. My vehicle bounced around so much I feared one of my tires was about to pop. Thank God for the car wash coupon I had sitting on top of my dashboard.

The slow speed didn't bother anybody except for me. I was the only person around for what seemed like miles. I kept looking in my rear view mirror, expecting to see a line of cars, trucks, or even tractors all waiting for me to kick it up a notch. But no. Absolutely nothing. I tossed around the description in my head of what I would have to tell an operator at AAA if they had to come and tow my car. Of course, there wasn't any cell service, so I suppose that's a moot point. Anyone who travels frequently knows it's a bizarre feeling to have no idea where you are, even at 9:00 in the morning.

As I finally pulled up to the property, several official trucks from Arkansas State University were in a small parking lot next door. Crews were putting final touches on the refurbished house.

ASU led the effort in restoring this historic piece of property, where Johnny Cash lived until he graduated high school. I had arrived a few days before it opened to the public or even the media. Only the immediate family members of the Cash family had seen it at this point. My schedule didn't allow me to join their grand opening celebration, so I decided to stop by a few days early, just to get a glance at the front of the house.

After introducing myself to the crew on site, they told me to "go on in" and that the door was open. They didn't have to tell me twice!

The before and after photos of the property are incredible to compare. The house was in awful condition and the construction crews miraculously brought it back to life. There's a mix of original flooring and furnishings and some other period pieces that didn't actually belong to the Cash family. The piano in the front room is in fact the same piano that was played by Johnny's mother. The books on the piano are original as well.

If you've seen the film *Walk The Line*, you'll be mesmerized as you walk from room to room, seeing first-hand the images you'll recognize from the movie. The small bedroom where Cash and his brother slept and the living room where the old radio sat are both featured throughout the movie. The family lived here from 1935 to 1954.

Over the years, tourists would become aware that the house still existed and would drive by to see it. When they approached, they'd see an old, partially boarded up, rather depressing-looking piece of property. The only problem was that when Cash lived there, the home was in great shape, even brand new. Tourists were getting the wrong impression of the star's childhood days. Shortly after I arrived, a couple on vacation from Spain stopped by to catch a glimpse of their own. Talk about a quick reminder of how far great music can spread.

The Dyess home was part of a 1930s program developed during the Depression by FDR. Farmers were given land, a mule, a small home, and money to buy food and plant crops. If they were successful, they would pay back the government. Cash certainly wasn't wealthy, and times were tough, but the refurbished home gives a much better representation of his life than it did before.

The property cost Arkansas State University $100,000. Then they poured at least that much money in concrete alone, as the house was sinking into the ground. Today, it serves as a beautiful reminder that greatness in America can be achieved from anywhere, even along an old and dirty, bumpy road.

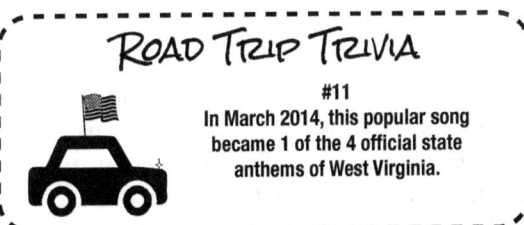

Road Trip Trivia

#11
In March 2014, this popular song became 1 of the 4 official state anthems of West Virginia.

CLYDESDALES FOR CHRISTMAS

Growing up in St. Louis, it was always neat to see the world-famous Budweiser Clydesdales featured on television ads or in parades all over the country. Anheuser-Busch, easily the most famous company to be founded in my hometown, has always had strong ties to the community. They offer free tours of the brewery, as well as free admission to their popular local wildlife park, Grant's Farm. Of course, the biggest connection has always been their sponsorship of the Cardinals baseball team, which they owned from 1953 to 1996.

If you live in St. Louis, or follow baseball closely, you know that there are several things you can count on for "Opening Day." Thousands of people wearing red, Stan Musial (until he died in 2013) making an appearance on the field, and the Budweiser Clydesdales parading around the entire field of the stadium. Each spring, these gentle giants gallop onto the warning track in the outfield while "Here Comes The King," the official Budweiser theme song, is played by the stadium's organist.

These days, the horses make appearances all over the country and can be found at Budweiser locations in several U.S. cities. But the tradition started here in St. Louis, something longtime residents don't mind pointing out. After all, the tagline on all of those beer commercials still reads "Anheuser-Busch, Saint Louis, Missouri."

Just about two hours west of the company's downtown headquarters is a place called Boonville. This small town of about 8,000 residents is home to Warm Springs Ranch, the breeding facility of the Budweiser Clydesdales. This is also the place where some of those heartwarming or humorous Super

Bowl commercials are filmed.

On my first road trip to the ranch, I took my dad along for the ride. We met John Soto, who is in charge of making sure the entire operation runs smoothly. He's the guy who gets the call in the middle of the night when one of the mares is about to give birth.

Learning about the entire process was absolutely fascinating. For starters, a device is sutured to the wall of the birthing canal with a piece of string to monitor any activity. When the hooves of a birthing foal push through the string, John gets an alarm on his cell phone. But not just any alarm. On a test run, he illustrates how the device works and seconds later, his phone is humming the same melody of horns you hear when a horse race is about to begin.

"When I hear that sound, I come running," says Soto, who lives on-site. He can be there—if need be—in about one minute.

With no public tours scheduled, we pretty much had the place to ourselves. First, we walked through the property's 25,000-square-foot barn, which is the headquarters of the breeding operation. Each horse has its own shelter, with its name displayed in big letters. Some are quite friendly, others couldn't care less that we were standing there, but all of them are about as laid back and chilled out as they could be.

We arrived a couple of weeks after the ranch's newest addition, Paris. Their names typically start with the first letter of their mother's name. The rest is determined by personality and a friendly debate among the staff. We learned how Paris came to get her name, but were sworn to secrecy.

Next stop was a look inside the trailers that serve as a home to the horses while on the road. Back when Anheuser-Busch first started using them for promotional purposes, they traveled by train. Their first trip was to Washington, DC to deliver beer to FDR, marking the end of Prohibition. The trailers are spacious, air-conditioned, and about as glamorous as animal accommodations go. They travel in the massive trailers and rest each night in stables strategically located along their route.

To be a Budweiser Clydesdale, there are specific requirements. They must be dark bay in color, have a white blaze, black mane and tail, and four white stocking feet. To make the cut for one of the traveling hitches, each horse goes through a complex training process. They must learn to deal with simple things like being bathed, and more complicated things like staying calm with loud noises or strangers approaching them.

Here at the ranch, the greatest part of the experience was simply being able to mingle among the couple of dozen young Clydesdales. Along with my dad, we walked through the gated entrance to one of the many pastures. The young horses were curious and within minutes, completely surrounded us. While they may technically be "toddlers," they weigh at least 200 pounds. Much like your cat that lays on your laptop the moment you want to check your e-mail, these young horses also have no concept of boundaries.

Though the thought of a fatal trouncing is always on your mind, it's impossible not to smile; these beautiful creatures just want to get close to you. As I lovingly pet one, three more are checking out the contents of the camera bag hanging on my shoulder. My dad, laughing aloud a couple yards away, spins in a circle to equally distribute affection to another group.

As our time on the ranch draws to an end, they follow us to the gate, where we say goodbye. Walking toward the parking lot, you can't help but look back over your shoulder to see them resting their heads on the gate.

"I want one for Christmas," says my dad.

Yeah, I'll get right on that.

100 MEN HALL

Seems strange to say now, but I found Bay St. Louis by accident. The southern Mississippi town, a short drive east of New Orleans, wound up on my radar only because of a scheduling conflict. Today I'd consider it one of my favorite small towns in America. Laid back, slower pace, and kind people.

On my first of many visits to the town, I met a woman named Kerrie Loya. She was the owner of a building known as the 100 Men D.B.A. Hall. For Kerrie and her husband, Jesse, the name of the property was pretty much the only thing they knew.

In the weeks following Hurricane Katrina, Jesse was a volunteer helping to clean up the colossal destruction that hit the Gulf Coast. Bay St. Louis received the brunt of that storm and caused incredible damage. The Loyas were no strangers to refurbishing buildings, mainly thanks to Jesse's construction background. The 100 Men D.B.A. Hall, only about a mile from the water, was for sale, despite having no doors, windows, or even a roof.

"Jesse called and said he wanted to buy it," says Kerrie. Noting the condition, and the fact that they were living in California at the time, she wasn't too enthused about owning a broken-down building. Several weeks later, Jesse rode his bike by the hall and noticed "R.O.E." spray-painted on the exterior wall. The letters stood for "right of entry," meaning the building was set to be knocked down by the Army Corps of Engineers.

In 1894, a group of residents drew up the bylaws for an organization called "The One Hundred Men Debating Benevolent Association." Its mission was to assist and take care of fellow members, not much different than a church or other social group. The difference being that, instead of donations or

MORE TO EXPLORE...
The 100 Men D.B.A. Hall is part of the Mississippi Blues Trail.

tithes, the group raised money largely by holding concerts.

In 1922, the original building was not enclosed, but more of a pavilion with a screened-in porch. It was indeed the social hot spot for mostly the black residents in the area and the place for weddings, parties, and, of course, music. When the group eventually fizzled and as ownership changed hands, its history was lost. Not so much a mystery, as some older residents still knew the stories, but more that nobody seemed to care.

As Jesse noted the impending destruction of the property, he again reached out to Kerrie who finally agreed that they would buy the building. "It was definitely a money pit," she noted more than once.

Each afternoon, Jesse was hard at work on the hall, tearing out damaged flooring, painting walls, repairing windows—whatever needed to be done. As word started to get around that these crazy Californians had bought the building, curious locals started to pop in. One took a look around at the condition and said to Jesse, "You know, I saw Ike and Tina Turner here." Another stopped by and said, "Etta James used to sing here all the time. Fats Domino, too."

Before too long, the Loyas learned that a long list of music legends had performed on the stage inside the 100 Men D.B.A. Hall. Artists like Ray Charles, Big Joe Turner, and The Claudettes were part of something called the "Chitlin Circuit," where black artists were booked at a string of venues along the coast, starting in New Orleans.

Working on the building wasn't exactly a fun project. To put it bluntly, Kerrie admits, "It wasn't fun at all." It was draining both financially and emotionally. Restoring a building under normal conditions is tough enough. Doing so in an area ravished by a hurricane is not a challenge most can face head-on.

The Loyas finally did finish their work on the building and

brought it back to near-perfect condition. More than 250 Bay St. Louis residents joined them for a party to celebrate. It was at this party where locals showed gratitude and appreciation for their efforts.

Shortly after, the 100 Men D.B.A. Hall was added to the Mississippi Blues Trail, which is a major tourism entity in the state, drawing interest from blues fans internationally. The recognition is particularly important as there are very few actual historical buildings still standing along the trail.

The Loyas recently sold the property and moved along to another adventure. "Every building has a story," says Kerrie. That's true. But probably not like the one at 303 Union Street.

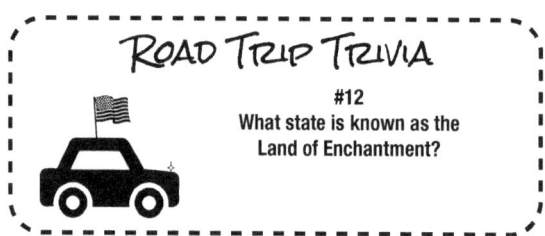

ROAD TRIP TRIVIA

#12
What state is known as the
Land of Enchantment?

MEETING THE MUPPETS

When I was a child, Kermit the Frog was my hero. Watching Jim Henson hosting *The Muppet Show*, his most popular creation, probably inspired me to become a host, entertainer, and broadcaster. The first toy I remember from my youth was a Kermit plush doll. I still have a wooden box with Kermit painted on it along with "Billy", the name everyone called me until I grew too mature for my own good and insisted on being named "Bill."

The Center For Puppetry Arts in Atlanta, Georgia, recently received an incredible donation from the family of Jim Henson. Over 500 artifacts, including original Muppet characters, are now part of the museum's permanent collection. The Jim Henson Collection is the latest addition to the museum that's known for telling the story of puppetry, both in the U.S. and around the world.

Curators with the museum say that people have been known to cry when they see the real Muppets up close. It's a special childhood link for most visitors. While I didn't personally shed any tears, I found myself in complete awe of seeing these characters that I've adored for so long in person.

"You're never leaving that place, are you?" was the reply text message from my brother when I sent him a photo of Kermit and me.

Like most things on television, the Muppets aren't nearly as big as you'd imagine. Even without the helping hand of a human to bring them to life, they still seem alive and full of personality.

Not all of the Muppets are out for visitors; in fact, just about a dozen of the full collection are displayed. This allows the center to keep things fresh by constantly rotating what's on display.

But the ones that they did select for the debut of the Henson Collection were perfect.

I saw Big Bird, Elmo, Bert and Ernie, Oscar the Grouch, and Grover. You'll also see Kermit, Miss Piggy, Scooter, Dr. Teeth, and the piano-playing dog Rawlf.

The Henson family also donated Jim's workspace, including a desk and other Muppet workshop tables and gadgets used while he was alive. Looking at the creative process is just as fun as seeing the final products. Mr. Henson would use all sorts of odd things to create the perfect puppets.

"The Henson family has always had a close connection to the center," according to Kelsey Fritz, who handles the exhibits here. Mr. Henson and Kermit the Frog were here to cut the ribbon when the building opened. The huge collection required some adjustments, including an expanded storage facility to handle all of the characters and other items.

Fans of *Fraggle Rock*, *Dark Crystal*, and other Henson productions won't be disappointed; you'll find characters from those series as well.

The most common phrase heard in the Henson collection? "Big Bird is such a big bird!" Sounds hilarious, but people are apparently stunned at just how big he is.

In addition to the Muppets on display, the Center For Puppetry Arts also features iconic puppet characters like Gumby, Punch and Judy, and cool one-of-a-kind artifacts, including a first model of costume pieces from *The Lion King*.

The Center also teaches young children about learning through puppetry. A very cool satellite TV production team interacts with school kids from all across the country. Students are able to create a puppet of their own and then play along with puppet masters who join them via satellite from Atlanta to put on an original show.

> here is a sense of our characters caring
> r each other and having respect for each
> her. A positive feeling ... of
> e. That's a key to eve...
>
> – Jim Henson

MORE TO EXPLORE...
Be sure to climb to the top of Stone Mountain while in Atlanta!

After conveying some of the good-natured ridicule from friends about my love of Muppets at this stage in life, Ms. Fritz adds, "You're never too old for puppets!" Turns out that's true—the Henson collection is most popular with folks who are older and grew up watching these beloved characters on television.

IT'S NEVER AS BAD AS THEY SAY IT IS

One afternoon in 2013, I was scrolling through Facebook and came across a headline that all of us have seen at least once: *These Are The Ten Worst States To Live In*. These days, I don't click on those stories. Back then, I didn't know better.

My home state of Missouri was listed among the ten. And, while the author of the piece had clearly never visited our state, it wasn't the listing that bothered me as much as the picture they used to represent the place I call home. If I had to pick one photograph to represent Missouri, I might choose the Gateway Arch, the beautiful fountains in Kansas City, or maybe an aerial view of the Ozarks in the fall.

Instead of the many great options that represent the Show Me State, the writer used a photo of a run-down trailer park. In the photo, a man wearing a sleeveless T-shirt is seen walking a couple of sick-looking dogs.

Helloooo, Missouri!

For several minutes, I just stopped and stared at this image. All I could think of was that most people with a lick of common sense would understand this doesn't represent our state. But I also knew that even if one or two people around the world were fooled, it was too many. This was the moment when I decided that I wanted to promote positive stories, and work to knock down ridiculous stereotypes that hamper many cities and states across the U.S. This was the exact moment that I decided to be a full-time travel journalist.

The national news media deserves a lot of blame for spreading incorrect narratives and persistent stereotypes. News reporters often blow into towns to cover stories, pretend like they really know the lay of the land, and then sprint to another destination,

leaving a public relations mess behind.

A few years ago, some major flooding near downtown Memphis, Tennessee, made the national news. It caused some local headaches for sure, but 95 percent of downtown was untouched. When viewers from across the country watched the news, they saw reporters on-site, with tightly edited video in their stories, making it look as though the entire city was under water. It wasn't.

In Ferguson, Missouri, the 2014 riots were devastating for the small suburban St. Louis municipality. Even more devastating was the media coverage that portrayed the entire region as being unsafe. It wasn't. I should know; I have lived most of my life in St. Louis County. Headlines like "St. Louis on Fire" were incredibly misleading.

Other media personalities, like talk show hosts or talking heads, often spout common myths about regions or share shaky statistics about individual cities. Anytime someone shares a statistic with you, remember this brilliant quote from author Ron DeLegge: "Ninety-nine percent of statistics only tell 49 percent of the story."

Of course, as easy as it is to blame the news media, we're sometimes just as guilty. Have you ever shared a story on Facebook that turned out to be untrue? Have you made a joke about a particular region of the country? Perhaps you've even talked down your own hometown.

In the winter of 2016, I was visiting Topeka, Kansas. It was part of a two-week road trip that was designed to show that Kansas, often the butt of many jokes, really does have things to see and do.

At the end of my first day in town, I was using the elevator to head back to my hotel room. The gentleman riding along with me asked what I was in town for. I told him that I was writing a travel story. Clearly a local, he rolled his eyes and scoffed, "Why? There's nothing to do here."

Not missing a beat, I opened my notepad, and began ticking off all of the things I had done over the course of one day, which restaurants I had checked out, and the people I had met. I then told him everything I had on my agenda for the next day. Bewildered, all the man could say was, "Huh."

Back when I first started traveling, I would share my list of upcoming travel destinations with friends to get their reactions or input. On one occasion, I mentioned Little Rock, Arkansas as one of my stops for a Southern road trip. One lady snickered and quickly pounced, announcing: "Oh, you don't want to visit there." She went on a rant about things she had heard or supposedly had seen online but admitted she actually had not spent any time there.

After she finished her rambling, I responded, "Okay. That settles it. I'm definitely going."

That summer, Little Rock instantly became one of my favorite cities. People were delightful, it was affordable, there were so many amazing places to eat, and there were lots of things to do. The River Market district is so much fun, with a sculpture garden and concert area. The bridges, lit at night with cool colors shining over the Arkansas River, are so beautiful!

During that visit, I became friends with a couple of wonderful women. I met both of them through interviews I had conducted for my radio show and on tours of the town. To this day, I remain good friends with both of them, and can count on their advice or a friendly voice when I need it most. I've been back to town several times to visit them. Both ladies joked recently that they think of me as a younger brother.

I often ponder the possibility that I never would have met them had I listened to the person who told me not to go to

Disregarding stereotypes has brought new friends into my life from all over America, including these from Little Rock, Arkansas.

Little Rock. After six years of covering travel and tourism, I've learned that most places are never as bad as people say they're going to be. I've learned that you can always find something positive if you're willing to look.

If you take away just one thing from this book, remember that 99 percent of us have more in common than you think. America is full of different ideas, perspectives, and personalities. That's a strength, not a weakness. Hit the road as often as you can, talk to complete strangers along the way, and keep your glass half full. Always.

ROAD TRIP TRIVIA ANSWERS

1. "God Bless The USA" (Lee Greenwood)
2. Thomas Jefferson
3. Vanna White
4. "American Pie" (Don McLean)
5. Las Vegas
6. Four: West Coast, Northern, Midwestern, and Southern
7. Philadelphia, Pennsylvania
8. Cheers
9. Bill Gates
10. Candlestick Park
11. "Take Me Home, Country Roads" (John Denver)
12. New Mexico

MORE TO EXPLORE...
After visiting the Opry, stop at Goo Goo Clusters Shop & Kitchen for a sweet treat.

On stage at the historic Grand Ole Opry in Nashville, Tennessee.

MY FAVORITE TRAVEL APPS

Airbnb

When a hotel just isn't an option or is too expensive, Airbnb is a great alternative. I've used it on road trips for last-minute accommodations or to find a place to crash for a short while. Pay close attention to the ratings and feedback. (Tip: Only stay at places that have had a lot of guests.) You're sure to meet some nice people, too!

Field Trip

Field Trip allows you to really get a sense of your surroundings by pointing out landmarks, important historical spots, or general information that you might not be aware of. The app can run in the background while you're driving and "cards" will pop up on your screen with details about things that fall into your selected categories. You can choose options like "Food & Drinks," "Cool & Unique," or "Arts & Museums." The cards can be narrated through your vehicle's Bluetooth capability.

iExit

We've all been driving down the highway and debating whether or not to exit for food and fuel, not knowing if an exit up ahead might have better, or fewer, options. With the iExit app you can see details about restaurants, stores, attractions, and gas stations—including current fuel prices. The GPS detects the highway, and the direction you're driving while listing the upcoming exits.

Just Ahead

If you like the idea of having your own personal tour guide, this is the perfect app for your next trip. Just Ahead can share an interesting story about something you see on the horizon, give you the background story on a small town, or list the highlights of a big city. All of the content is produced by travel writers from *National Geographic, AAA, Outside Magazine*, and others. All you have to do is look out the window and listen to the highlights.

Roadside America

Of all the travel apps I have on my phone, this is my favorite. Of course, I'm a big fan of pulling off the road and seeing things like the tallest fork in America. (Hello, Springfield, Missouri.) Roadside America has brilliantly archived nearly every quirky attraction in the country. When you open the app, a list of fun stops will show up based on the distance from your current location. Some are better than others, and a User Review feature rates the stops to let you know if they're worthy of a visit. There are eight versions available. You can opt to purchase the region you typically travel in or unlock all of the information at once.

Spot Hero

Finding a place to park, especially in a city you're not familiar with can be a huge hassle. Time that you spend looking for a spot can be stressful, and even cause you to be late for an important meeting. Park in the wrong spot, and you could wind up with a costly ticket —or worse. The Spot Hero app can tell you ahead of time where to find the most reasonable parking spot and, in many cases, you can pay in advance to reserve it.

INDEX

100 Men Hall, 107–110
Air Force One, 60
Al Johnson's Restaurant, 41
Alabama Gulf Coast Zoo, 46–49
Alabama, 47–49
American Sign Museum, 62
Atlanta, Georgia, 111–114
Arizona, 35–38
Arkansas, 63, 101, 118
Barker, Bob, 3
Baseball, 25
Bay St. Louis, Mississippi, 45, 107–110
Beartooth Scenic Byway, 50
Bolin, Jim, 92
Bradley Barn, 89
Bradley, Jerry, 89
Budweiser Clydesdales, 104–106
Bush, George W., 15
California, 33–34, 84
Camp Helen State Park, 7
Carney, Dan, 23–24
Carter, Jimmy, 15
Casey, Illinois, 92–94
Cash, Johnny, 101–103
Cato, Jack, 76–78
CBS, 33–34
Center For Puppetry Arts, 13, 62, 111–114
Chester, Illinois, 95-96

INDEX

Children's Museum of Indianapolis, 61
City Museum, 62
Clevlen, Rick, 26, 50
Colorado State University, 100
Cooperstown, New York, 25–26
Cracker Barrel, 76
Crystal Bridges Museum of Art, 63
Disney, Walt, 81–82
Door County, Wisconsin, 41
Doubleday Field, 28
Dr. Pepper, 16
Dude Rancher Lodge, 51
Dyes, Arkansas, 101–103
Eisenhower, Dwight, 79–80
Florida, 7
Fred Rogers Center, 56
Georgia, 111–114
Gettysburg, Pennsylvania, 12
Glore Psychiatric Museum, 16
Graceland, 81
Grand Canyon, 35
Hall, Patti, 47–49
Halloween, 29
Hearing Aid Museum, 11
Heinz History Center, 53
Henry Ford Museum, 62
Hiking, 35–38
House On The Rock, 82

INDEX

Hurricane Katrina, 45
Illinois, 92–96
Jefferson City, Missouri, 85–88
Jennings, Waylon, 90–91
Jones, George, 97–99
Joplin, Missouri, 43
Kansas, 22–24, 117
Kentucky, 83-84
Kermit The Frog, 13, 111–114
Knievel, Evel, 12
Lane, Griff, 9
Lane's Barber Shop, 9
Lebanon, Tennessee, 77–78
Levensen, Barry, 12
Liston, Sonny, 85
Little Rock, Arkansas, 118
Louisville, Kentucky, 84
Memphis, Tennessee, 81
Michigan, 3, 39-40, 64
Miller, Ray, 85
Mississippi, 9–10, 18–21, 45, 70, 107–110
Missouri, 7–8, 16, 43–45, 62, 85–88, 115
Missouri State Penitentiary, 85
Mister Ed's Elephant Museum, 12
Montana, 50-53
Motown Records, 3, 39
Musial, Stan, 25
Nashville, Tennessee, 97

INDEX

National Museum of Play, 13, 61
National Museum of the United States Air Force, 60, 63
National Museum of Toys and Miniatures, 13, 61
National Mustard Museum, 11
National WWII Museum, 61
New York, 13, 25–28
Oklahoma City, Oklahoma, 16
Oxford, Mississippi, 70
Panama City Beach, Florida, 7
Pennsylvania, 12, 54–56, 79
Pittsburgh, Pennsylvania, 55–56, 120
Pizza Hut, 22
Playboy Playmate of the Year, 66
Popeye, 95–96
Presley, Elvis, 81
Rogers, Fred, 54–56
Saint Louis, Missouri, 7, 62
San Jose, California, 84
Secret Service, 31
Sesame Street, 13, 111–114
Sleeping Bear Dunes, 64
South Dakota, 72–75
Sportsman's Park, 25
Springfield, Missouri, 11
Tabasco, 14
Tennessee, 77, 81, 89, 90–91, 97–99, 117, 122
Texas, 15
The Muppet Show, 13, 111–114

INDEX

The Price Is Right, 33
The White House, 30
Topeka, Kansas, 117
Tunica History Museum, 9
Tunica, Mississippi, 9
Waco, Texas, 16
Warm Springs Ranch, 104–106
Washington, DC, 31–32
Wichita State University, 23
Wichita, Kansas, 23
Winchester Mystery House, 84
Wisconsin, 11, 41–42, 82
Wonder, Stevie, 39
World of Coca-Cola, 16

www.ingramcontent.com/pod-product-compliance
Lightning Source LLC
Chambersburg PA
CBHW050324120526
44592CB00014B/2039